The Roughwood Book of Pickling

Homestyle Recipes for Chutneys, Pickles, Relishes, Salsas, and Vinegar Infusions

William Woys Weaver

Photographs by Noah Fecks

RIZZOLI
NEW YORK

New York Paris London Milan

For Alain Passard, visionary chef of Arpège,
a generous host, and master of *éphémères du jour*.

The Roughwood Book of Pickling

**Homestyle Recipes for Chutneys, Pickles, Relishes,
Salsas, and Vinegar Infusions**

First published in the United States of America in 2019 by
Rizzoli International Publications, Inc.
300 Park Avenue South
New York, NY 10010
rizzoliusa.com

Photography: Noah Fecks
noahfecks.com

Publisher: Charles Miers
Editor: Jono Jarrett
Design: Jennifer S. Muller
Production Manager: Colin Hough-Trapp
Managing Editor: Lynn Scrabis

Printed in China
2019 2020 2021 2022 / 10 9 8 7 6 5 4 3 2 1

ISBN: 978-0-7893-3678-1
Library of Congress Control Number: 2019931789

Visit us online:
Facebook.com/RizzoliNewYork
Twitter: @Rizzoli_Books
Instagram.com/RizzoliBooks
Pinterest.com/RizzoliBooks
Youtube.com/user/RizzoliNY
Issuu.com/Rizzoli

Contents

Introduction

The Story of Roughwood

This book was composed in my kitchen garden at Roughwood, inspired by the amazing array of rare fruits and vegetables that have given my life unique direction over the past fifty years. When I moved my grandfather's 1930s seed collection in the 1970s, to my house and kitchen garden in Devon, Pennsylvania, little did I realize this would open a new chapter in the collection's ongoing evolution, while at the same time launch my own career as an author and food historian. On the other hand, when you assume oversight of a national treasure like the Roughwood Seed Collection—a miniaturized universe of heirloom plants and their unique stories—it soon becomes imperative to share that experience with all the like-minded cooks and horticulturists beyond Roughwood's garden fence.

Let us begin with a little history. What is known today as the Roughwood Seed Collection began as my grandfather's two-acre kitchen garden in West Chester, Pennsylvania, around 1932. H. Ralph Weaver (1896–1956) was a semi-professional horticulturist (with emphasis on professional) whose main line of work was his accounting firm, but his heart was always in his garden. He took up his overalls and hoe as a means to sustain his wife and family as well as many less fortunate relatives through the Great Depression. Although money was tight, the family managed well enough, and through word of mouth my grandfather's garden became legendary for feeding the many without consideration of cost or compensation. Four hundred quarts of tomato sauce one year; ninety quarts of pickled peaches another—entirely from the bounty of the garden. The cellar was full of canning jars, and truth be told, thirty years later some of them remained unopened.

I grew up at my grandfather's knee and from him came to understand that the Green World around us is a marvelous place. He was a Pennsylvania Dutch *Braucher*, an herbal healer, and the last in his line who could trace that oral tradition all the way back to the ancient highlands of Switzerland where our family originated. For that reason, he was fascinated with our genealogy and his inherited role as a Green Man and master of natural cures. His garden was his kingdom and his apothecary, and even as a precocious little boy with annoying streams of questions, I soon learned how important his beehives were in making certain the cherry trees produced cherries, the apple trees their apples, and everything else on those two acres of vegetables, all was dependent on Nature's largesse.

He was a true visionary who bio-diversified long before the concept existed, let alone came into vogue. Sustainability was his unspoken rule of thumb: Racing pigeons provided nutrient-rich manure for the gardens and bees from his beehives pollinated the fruit trees. Working on the Weaver family genealogy, my grandfather used Lancaster County family connections to add heirloom seeds grown in the Dutch Country for many generations. Local folk artist Horace Pippin struck up a friendship with my grandfather and became a regular at his lunch table, trading seeds for beestings, a common folk remedy at the time, to mitigate the pain of a World War I injury. Many of those seeds, including the rare fish pepper, are now considered historically significant within African-American culinary culture.

While my grandfather's untimely death in 1956 brought an abrupt end to his chapter of the story, it didn't end there. Some ten years later, while I was a student at the University of Virginia, I discovered his seed collection in a bottom drawer of my grandmother's deep freezer—my grandfather had known that by freezing, seeds could be stored for a long time, so by this stroke of luck, many of his most valuable seeds were still viable. By the mid-1970s, I had brought most of his original garden back under cultivation, and in 1979, I moved the seed collection to my home in Devon, Pennsylvania. Since the collection had no official name, I dubbed it the Roughwood Seed Collection after the name given to the property in the 1880s by Philadelphia banker Thomas Alexander Biddle. While sounding dignified in a Main Line–socialite way, there was always a certain joke behind the name—Biddle bought what was then a seventy-five-acre farm as a secluded retreat (read: love nest) for a certain Mrs. Puter, his mistress and a notorious madam infamous for her leather corsets and whips. No old house is without its ghosts and scandals!

My own pickling experiments expanded as the Roughwood Seed Collection grew to include more and more unusual vegetables and fruits. When I acquired seeds for rare peppers from Peru, I wanted to know how the Peruvians used them, or how *chiles congos* were cooked in Central America. This required finding local Spanish-language cookbooks in order to discover the secrets of their regional cuisines. On and on the learning curve went until now I am as much at home with Andean salsas as I am with unique Indian chutneys, or salted vegetables from rare corners of the Eastern Mediterranean. By degrees I created a collection of working recipes and they form the basis for this book.

Furthermore, throughout the book I employ ingredients from my garden, the fresher the better—for example, for best texture, cucumbers must be pickled the same morning you harvest them. Also keep in mind that vegetables raised organically will keep better than produce fertilized with chemicals. I have had organic cucumbers hold forth in a cool closet for as long as six months with no sign of spoiling. That is why I urge you to use organic produce in your pickles: Chemical fertilizers, like spigot water laced with antibiotics, will cause your pickles to degrade more quickly. This is also why commercial pickles contain so many preservatives—one infusion of chemicals to counterbalance the negative effects of the others. My pickles are what I call "natural pickles," in that they rely only on natural ingredients to make them succeed.

Happily, with more than seven thousand heirloom varieties of vegetables and food plants now at Roughwood, there is no shortage of interesting and challenging ingredients. But do not be put off by heirloom varieties not seen in supermarkets—supermarket produce is not good for pickling anyway because it is generally too old and flabby. I will suggest likely substitutes, or even better, you can order seeds directly from Roughwood, Baker Creek Heirloom Seeds, or the other seed companies listed among the sources on page 199. You can have the pleasure of growing your own ingredients and judging for yourself what a difference that freshness makes.

My grandfather once told me with a wink that each of his bees had a name. He was pulling my leg, of course, yet his point should be well taken: We must respect all the living things around us, and that respect was carried into the kitchen where my grandmother took over the process. To my childhood eyes, she wrought marvelous changes to everything that passed through her hands. The ancient Greeks had a word, *chrysoheres*, or "golden hands," as though guided by divine powers, and who is to say they weren't? I call it Granny's Touch.

Granny's Touch

My grandmother Grace Hickman was born in 1900 on a large farm along Pocopson Creek in Chester County, Pennsylvania. Grace's father operated a family business out of a nearby slaughterhouse, where all manner of pork products were made, including the scrapple for which the Hickman family was justly well known. Her mother, Esther, cooked six days a week making pies, baked goods, and pickles for sale at the West Chester Farmer's Market (sadly now the site of a parking garage) and at Reading Terminal Market in Philadelphia.

Before marrying Grace's father, Esther Hannum attended Sarah Tyson Rorer's Philadelphia Cooking School with a bevy of her Quaker friends in the city. That professional training and a penetrating intellect lifted her several notches above the ordinary home cook, and she threw herself into experimental cookery with special gusto. Later in life, Esther was always remembered as an exacting cook, and I have one of her manuscript cookbooks to prove it.

Grace spent most of her time with her father as his presumptive heir-in-training, and proved a better shot with the slaughterhouse pistols than most men. A tomboy at heart, she did not learn basic cooking as a young girl, but did learn to pickle because, as she later confessed, "it came naturally." When it came to pickling, Grace cooked boarding-house style, which was not altogether surprising, as that's how Esther had cooked. And, during hard times, having a larder overflowing with laid-in supplies was like having money in the bank. One's own handiwork always tasted better than canned food from the store, not to mention that you knew exactly what was in it. That dimension was always a leitmotif to any discussion of food at the family table, as my grandfather had a weak heart since childhood, so a careful diet and fresh food were an integral part of his routine—that and a shot of rye whiskey each evening almost up until the day he died.

That family pickling bug also proved especially helpful after Grace's older sister died unexpectedly from complications from childbirth. Since her sister's husband was not capable of supporting his children, Grace rolled up her sleeves and did the Quaker thing by moving her family back east to Pennsylvania from Minnesota, where my grandfather had just finished college. Together with her younger sister, Myrtle, Grace raised money to support their nieces and nephews by organizing formal teas in an old stone house in Downingtown, where local ladies could socialize, play bridge, and enjoy an array of refreshments—including a veritable buffet of Grace and Myrtle's homemade pickles. By the 1940s, using Grace and Myrtle's recipes, The Old Tea House had become a local culinary landmark recommended by Duncan Hines.

Thus it was my grandmother who taught me what she had learned about pickling from her own mother. Esther's prized handwritten pickle book was accidentally lost many years later during a fit of overzealous helpfulness on the part of my mother and aunt, who decided one day to help Grace clean and reorganize her kitchen. During the ensuing dust storm, the pickle book and the manuscript cookbook of my great-great-grandmother Barbara Weaver (along with her diary of an 1878 tour of Europe) both disappeared, never to be seen again. After the cleaning committee left, I discovered Grace weeping quietly at a table cluttered with the useless things her daughters-in-law had considered too good to throw out. The handwritten pickle book was gone. The unique Weaver family cookbook, several hundred pages thick, was also gone.

This family drama would not be pertinent were it not for the fact that, many years later, when I began to replant my grandfather's garden in West Chester, Grace responded by verbalizing old recipes and retelling their stories. My grandfather's ancient gnarly sage bushes were still alive then, and when she told me it was the sage in Scrapple Sauce (page 174) that complemented the flavor of scrapple, the whole pickling narrative began to unfold. Soon my grandmother was trotting me through Philadelphia pepper hash, corn relish, salting techniques for sauerkraut, the sweets-and-sours of chow-chow, and innumerable little insights that she had picked up over the years while processing the bounties of her own kitchen garden.

Food does not stand still in a historical timeline, nor do pickles. I had reassured Grace that day at the table that the missing cookbooks meant nothing, because the best of what they contained was still in her head. I promised her that I would create a new pickle book, because each generation must have its own. Thus the book I have created here is not drawn on the collection of heirloom family recipes long lost to the county dump, but from the living ingredients in my own kitchen garden processed with the blessings of Granny's Touch. Even the recipes that do come from Esther, such as Five-Bean Chow-Chow (page 128), Gooseberry Chutney (page 129), and Spicy Yellow Tomato Catsup (page 64), have been adjusted to agree with modern sensibilities, and my sensibilities in particular. I suppose it is fair to say that I have inherited Grace's passion for pickling, and for reasons only known

to my Creator, I seem to have acquired her touch. Where I differ from my grandmother is that I have my father's taste for hot and spicy—Grace was terrified of anything resembling cayenne pepper; even paprika was treated gingerly.

I spent the formative years of my childhood in my grandfather's garden and in Grace's kitchen, so it probably is fair to say that I learned to pickle as soon as I learned to use a hoe and shovel. I also learned the core meaning of generosity, or "living *above* money," as my grandmother expressed it. Today my spiritual family consists of a marvelous adoptive community composed of thousands of readers who have taken their lead and inspiration from my many books and the Roughwood Seed Collection. Judging from the letters, e-mails, messages, and, on occasion, surprise visits from kindred spirits, my grandfather's unpretentious mission has touched many lives in a positive way.

It is my hope that this book, which reflects my grandmother's hitherto untold side of the Roughwood story, will likewise prove to be a nurturing presence in the kitchen. However, this is not a beginner's handbook—those are common enough already. Here, I am assuming you know how to cook, and perhaps have already tried your hand at pickling. All the same, the recipes in this collection should open up new worlds of flavors and exciting ways to change common things into edible memories. The expertise that went into this book represents the accumulated knowledge of several generations of family cooks, as we have always been concerned with the notion that good food from the garden deserves good treatment in the kitchen. That underlying mantra is what my grandmother called the "Quaker thing," truth speaking through the quality of one's deeds. On that note, let this guidebook to creative home pickling be your talisman for success, as you may discover good gardening and proficiency at pickling have always gone hand in hand. More important, the spirituality of your relationship to your garden and to where your food comes from will open insights into well-being and a happy connectedness to place.

—William Woys Weaver, "Epicure with Hoe"
Roughwood, Devon, Pennsylvania

How to Use This Book

This is a book for those with basic cooking experience, although to be quite honest, there is indeed a range of recipes from very simple and easy to more complex. My pickle recipes are arranged into three groups: Hot and Spicy, Salted or Fermented, and Sweet and Sour, plus a fourth chapter on vinegar infusions. That breakout felt like the best way to organize them, as those basic flavor categories more or less suggest how the pickles will be used in recipes or on the table. As my consumption of meat has declined (I gave up red meat many years ago), my consumption of pickles has increased. I use them with lentils, with stir-fries, as a sandwich filling, or simply as dips with bread. Like the Japanese tradition of enjoying a good pickle with a bowl of rice as a light meal, a larder full of pickles allows you to create instant meals without a microwave, for a snack or lunch, dinner on the hoof, or whatever works during a busy day in the garden.

Isabel Bermudez, my longtime housekeeper and the true guardian angel of Roughwood, not only supplied me with several rare peppers now in the collection, she also taught me how to make *pebre*, the national salsa of Chile (page 25). On that note, I have introduced a number of recipes using huacatay (*Tagetes minuta*), a South American relative of the common garden marigold, and several other Andean favorites, peppers like the golden yellow *aji amarillo* and *aji limó* (pepper

of Lima) and several delightful rarities. The other South American–inspired recipes, in particular in the Hot and Spicy chapter, are so different from typical American pickles, so flavorful in surprising ways, and yet brilliantly practical to make and keep, that once you try them you will always want to have a supply in the pantry in the event of an unexpected onslaught of hungry visitors. Also found throughout are recipes inspired by traditional American ingredients, old-time produce like blood peaches, fish peppers, martynias (also called devil's claws), and even green (unripe) blueberries. The eye of the pickle cook is constantly ranging through the garden to see what sorts of things can be salvaged or recycled, and I have invoked my late grandmother's savvy in the recipe for Zucchini Corn Relish (page 67), not to mention three heirloom classics: Jamaican-Style Chutney for Barbecue (page 37), Pepper Sherry (page 38), and Pepper Vinegar (page 40) from the 1848 Pennsylvania Dutch cookbook *Die Geschickte Hausfrau* (The Handy Housewife)—all of which only goes to prove that some heirloom recipes have achieved "thereness" (to quote Gertrude Stein), with no further improvement needed.

I remember years ago my grandmother and I visited an eighteenth-century farmhouse in Lancaster County. There was a summer kitchen attached where most of the pickling had been done, and, underneath, a set of stairs cut from the living rock led down into a spacious limestone cave lined with wooden shelves. It was chilly down there, the perfect natural refrigerator for food storage. Everyone who is serious about pickling should have something like this, even if it is just a secondhand refrigerator set off in a mudroom. Some pickles are best left unsealed so that you can access them as needed; thus a refrigerator will be essential, especially if you are making quantities for a large household.

I would recommend a large windowless, unheated closet or pantry room for the storage of your pickles. If you can line the floor and walls with ceramic tiles, so much the better—they will keep the space cool and are easy to scrub down during seasonal cleaning. Shelving that will accommodate tall crocks will also provide you with a place to put preparations like sauerkraut while they ferment. What you want is a space that does not provide easy access to fruit flies, which are the bane of warm-weather pickling, especially where fermentation is involved. Your approach to home pickling will hinge in some manner on the type of storage space you have.

Before proceeding to the recipes, I'd like to note that it is important to be as exacting as possible in everything you do. This means taking special care with the ingredients—this alone can be what makes a good pickle. Where water is called for, use only spring water free of impurities. Tap water can ruin a good pickle, in particular ferments, not only because it is treated, but also because it probably contains antibiotics. Second, use only the best grade of organic sugar—vegan sugar is the best choice (there are several reputable brands), although it is not cheap. Unlike commercial sugar, vegan sugar is not processed with ground animal bones, or "calcium," to keep the sugar loose. Sugar refineries exploit a loophole in food regulations by declaring bone dust as calcium, but like aluminum in baking powder, it will affect the outcome of a recipe, and if you care about animal bones or impurities in your food, you may want to know where that "calcium" came from.

On another level, I have discovered that vegan sugar also gives food, especially fruit, a much cleaner and "brighter" flavor. It is noticeable when you taste commercial pickles beside homemade pickles, and even my students at Drexel University, where I taught food studies, were amazed at the difference. Of course, the key thing here is

flavor enhancement. Flavor is like color: It is expressed in clear tonalities. Freshness applies to spices as well: Check the dates on the packages and purchase only the freshest. When making chutneys, be certain to grind all the spices the same day you intend to use them. That is why fresh Indian-style chutneys and curries have such outstanding flavor when made the traditional way. While on the subject of spices and dried herbs, I think one of the best suppliers in the trade is the Penn Herb Company in Philadelphia (PennHerb.com). This firm has been in business since the 1920s, they ship all over the United States, and they have one of the most extensive inventories of rare herbs and spices, even hard-to-find wild harvest herbs from unusual corners of the United States.

Another critical point is the salt you use: There are commercial salts called "pickling salts" (it should say this on the label), but basic kosher sea salt is likely the most reliable because it does not contain additives that will affect the outcome, especially for the salty-fermented pickles, and that's what I use. The absolute, hands-down best salt for pickling (and the brand I prefer) is produced by the J.Q. Dickinson Salt-Works in Malden, West Virginia, a family-owned business for seven generations that processes salt from a prehistoric sea. Their artisanal salt is free of pollutants and is preferred by many chefs who are passionate about sourcing.

However, it is my educated guess that sugar has won the pickling turf war because of the number of recipes today in which sugar figures all too prominently. Popular sweet-and-sour combinations, which originate in medieval cuisine, were not as sweet then as today. Industrialization and the canning revolution in the 1860s brought us glass jars with screw-top lids and easier methods for putting up food. Vacuum sealing in glass meant that salt and acid could be reduced in favor of sugar. For certain, as long as sugar remains cheap, it will outweigh healthier ingredients, especially now that high-fructose corn syrup is working its way into commercial recipes. In my own recipes, I have cut back on the sugar. Let's emphasize the fresh ingredients.

For best results, have on hand a special *batterie de cuisine* dedicated to pickling and preserving. These pans, tools, and utensils should not be used for anything else because meats and fish can leave trace flavors that will show up in unexpected and unwanted ways—

especially in recipes in which you are trying to achieve your own highly focused flavor combinations. The following is a basic list of equipment to keep on hand for creative pickling. Like many professional chefs, I prefer stainless steel products from All-Clad Metalcrafters of Canonsburg, Pennsylvania—we are lucky to have them in the Keystone State! Stainless steel is easy to clean and does not interact with acids, so you can use it without worrying about invasive flavors.

- Large microwave oven, preferably at least 1,250W. It should be roomy enough to accommodate 1-quart (1-liter) or even 1-gallon (4-liter) canning jars, so you can heat 4 to 6 jars in one batch

- 12-quart (12-liter) stainless steel multi-cooker or stockpot for sealing jars, if you prefer the water bath method

- 4-quart (4-liter) stainless steel or enameled cast-iron saucepan or small Dutch oven for cooking ingredients

- 3-quart (3-liter) saucepan for sterilizing lids and rings

- Stainless steel sieves and colanders (various sizes) for rinsing and draining ingredients

- Stainless steel measuring cups and measuring spoons

- Stainless steel slotted spoon with a plastic or rubberized handle

- Pair of tongs with rubberized handles for lifting lids and hot jars out of boiling water

- Wooden and stainless steel spoons or spatulas for stirring ingredients

- Large digital scale with imperial and metric calibrations, capable of measuring up to 10 pounds (5kg)

- Small digital scale with sensitive imperial and metric calibrations for measuring weights under 10 ounces (315g)

- Canning jars of various sizes (brand of your choice, such as Ball or Kerr)—make certain they are marked microwave-proof, as heirloom (pre-1960s) canning jars may look quaint, but they will most likely crack or explode if heated in a microwave

- 2-quart (2-liter) food processor or blender—I prefer a Vitamix because it has a remarkably strong motor

- Disposable latex gloves for handling hot peppers

- A Gulife oven glove (gulife-home.com), which prevents scalds or burns but permits dexterity when handling hot jars or large pots of boiling water

No matter what sealing method you plan to use (microwave or water bath), maintain absolute cleanliness in the kitchen. Run all your jars and equipment through the dishwasher to clean them thoroughly and keep on hand a number of freshly laundered washcloths so that you can wipe up spills or clean the jars of excess moisture, in particular on the rims, otherwise you may not obtain a perfect seal. These few precautions taken in advance will ensure that your pickling runs smoothly and successfully.

In many ways, home pickling is not as exacting as canning meats because many pickles are perfectly stable at ambient temperatures, making sealing often just an extra precaution. If you are making pickles commercially, then of course you must follow relevant laws and health department regulations to the letter. Until the advent of the microwave oven, home pickling relied on what is known as the water bath technique: Canning jars filled with hot pickles are covered tightly with lids and rings, then submerged in gently boiling water for a given amount of time in order to create a vacuum seal. The cooking time depends on the contents and the size of the jars. For this method you need large stockpots, racks for the jars, tongs for removing them, and an accurate timer—plus patience and precision. My grandmother used this technique faithfully in spite of the fact that pickling mostly occurred during the dog days of August and the entire house was thus transformed into a steam bath.

The late Jeanne Lesem, whose *Preserving Today* (1992) I recommend as useful and still timely reading, broke out of the old mold and came up with newer yet just as efficient ways to seal those jars. She was working out of a New York City apartment and had none of the luxuries of extra space that we have in our Pennsylvania farmhouses. During the time I helped her research her book, she put me on to the method of using the microwave to seal jars. It works, not to mention that the microwave also sterilizes, so I adopted that MO and kissed the steam bath goodbye.

Note that exact cooking times will depend on how powerful your microwave is and the size of the jars. Four square pint (500-ml) jars usually will fit even in a small microwave oven; if you wish to process 2-quart (2-liter) jars, which I often use for certain kinds of pickles, you may need a large, professional-size microwave as recommended above. Breaking down the sealing process into two or three runs also takes the pressure away from having to worry about a large batch of jars all at once. If you use French or Italian canning jars with metal clamps and rubber sealers, you will have to use the water bath method because these elements cannot be microwaved.

Master Method For Microwave Sealing:

Rather than repeat these instructions each time in the following recipes, when I instruct "seal (see page 17)," this is what I mean. You can also use a traditional water bath if you prefer; however, when using a microwave to reheat and then seal your jars, heating time is generally cut in half or more, thus a 10-minute water bath can become a 4-minute step in the microwave. Best of all, you do not heat up the kitchen— not to mention you'll cut down on water consumption!

Note: It's the flipping that is crucial for creating the vacuum seal. The microwave restores any temperature lost transferring the pickle mixture into jars more efficiently and safely than a hot water bath; therefore, in recipes where the mixture is already boiling hot going into the jars, the microwave step itself can be skipped and the filled jars are immediately turned upside-down for vacuum sealing.

Sterilize the jar(s), lid(s), and ring(s) in a large pot of lightly boiling water. This is a good first step, but try not to do this too far in advance, as you want the jar hot for filling.

Pack the pickle into the prepared jar(s) as directed in the recipe—if raw-packed, pour the hot brine over the pickles—then set the jars in a microwave-safe baking dish.

Transfer the baking dish to the microwave. Fill the dish half-full with hot water.

Microwave on high (100% power) just until the contents of the jars visibly bubble, 4 to 6 minutes, or more, depending on the size of the jars and the power of your microwave.

Carefully remove the hot jars from the microwave. Top the jars with the lids and screw the rings on tightly.

Turn the closed jars upside-down and let stand for 5 minutes, then return upright and let cool. Within 5 to 10 minutes, you should hear the pop indicating the seal was successful; you will know the seal is good when the lid is flat and does not press down when touched.

Any jars not successfully sealed after turning upright should be kept in the refrigerator and used within 2 weeks.

01

Hot and Spicy

Hot and spicy was not exactly the *métier* of my grandmother's generation. Home economics teachers championed paprika because it was little more than a bland, red garnish. Curry was about as daring as things got. Fortunately, American cookery has undergone a rebirth since then and, now that our green markets are overflowing with unusual hot and spicy ingredients, the time has come to learn how to use them.

Since I am mostly vegetarian (not strictly), I have always been partial to South Indian cooking especially the condiments, and having fresh herbs and spices (I grow my own cardamom) has left me spoiled when it comes to opening a jar of imported chutney. Jars of oily condiments with long lists of salty preservatives on the labels have always left me cold—fully disappointed by the price, first, then by the weak or smothered flavors of the contents. In many of the recipes I have created crossovers between continents—South American peppers in Indian pickles, for example. Food history does not stand still. It reflects an ongoing social evolution. And anyway, hot is hot. If you like spicy, this chapter will give you the culinary toys to make that happen in your own kitchen. For my potential critics who may want to dwell too much on geographical authenticity, may I ask one pointed question? Where were peppers in India before the discovery of the New World? The beauty of truly original cookery or cooking outside the box (figuratively and literally) is that we can take from the best and move the art of cuisine into new zones of creative discovery.

Bengali Green Chile Pickle

The purpose of this recipe is to supply the table with a spicy yet fragrant garnish or addition to stir-fries, rice dishes, or stewed meats. The peppers are excellent when sliced and scattered over main course dishes, and the flavorful brine can be used in salads or marinades. That said, this recipe is hot, very hot. If that is an issue, move on to another or go to the Sweet and Sour chapter (page 119). For this recipe, I prefer to use the Mexican *chile de rata*, which measures about ¼ inch (6mm) in diameter, but any long, narrow Thai or Indian hot pepper will work just as well. For extra eye appeal, mix ripe red peppers with the green ones; for additional flavor, grill the peppers before pickling them.

Yield: 1 quart (1 liter)

8 ounces (250g) long, pencil-thin hot green peppers, trimmed and cut into 3-inch (7.5-cm) lengths

1 large garlic clove, cut lengthwise into 4 or 5 slices

½ lime, cut in half lengthwise, seeded, and sliced

¼ cup (60ml) safflower oil or mustard oil

2 teaspoons caraway seeds

2 teaspoons whole cumin seeds

2 teaspoons whole anise seeds

2 teaspoons black mustard seeds

1 teaspoon whole ajwain seeds

3 cups (750ml) distilled white vinegar

½ cup (125g) organic sugar

1 tablespoon (15g) kosher sea salt

Sterilize the jar(s), lid(s), and ring(s) in a saucepan of lightly boiling water.

Pack the peppers standing on end in the prepared jar(s). Make certain they are packed tightly enough so they won't move when the brine is added.

In a small nonreactive preserving pan, heat the oil over medium heat and add the caraway, cumin, anise, mustard, and ajwain seeds. Stir and allow the spices to foam up for about 1 minute.

Add the vinegar, sugar, and salt, bring to a rolling boil, and boil for 2 minutes. Pour over the peppers and seal (see page 17). Store in a cool, dark place for up to 1 year. Refrigerate after opening.

Bihari Cucumber Chutney

Northern India is blessed with a plethora of unusual cucumbers, a fact that became abundantly clear when I came across a local Bihari cookbook brimming with one-of-a-kind cucumber recipes. The Indian variety used here has netted skin when mature, but when young the skin is brown, giving the chutney its unique mottled appearance. You can use whatever type of small pickling cucumber you prefer, or better yet, mix cornichons of different colors. After testing this recipe several times over the years, I would recommend that you choose peppers with special punch for the best flavor: The chutney loses something without ramped-up heat. Serve with rice or cooked whole wheat in place of meat. Leftover chutney liquid may be used as a marinade for duck, goose, or squab.

Yield: 2 quarts (2 liters)

2 pounds (1kg) firm pickling cucumbers, cut into small dice

1 pound (500g) green tomatoes, cut into small dice

2½ tablespoons (38g) kosher sea salt, divided

4 ounces (125g) carrot, pared and cut into 1-inch (2.5-cm) matchsticks

1 pound (500g) peeled and pitted unripe mango (weight after peeling and pitting), cut into small dice

½ cup (200g) freshly grated ginger

½ cup (90g) minced hot peppers, or to taste

¼ cup (60ml) virgin (cold-pressed) sesame oil

2 tablespoons (20g) black mustard seeds

1 tablespoon (10g) cumin seeds

2 tablespoons (10g) ground coriander

1 tablespoon (10g) whole Lucknow fennel seeds or Chinese fennel seeds

1 teaspoon ground mace

1 teaspoon ground star anise

3 cups (750ml) distilled white vinegar

1½ cups (375g) organic sugar

5 tablespoons (125g) tamarind pulp (picked of seeds or seed fragments)

Grated zest of 2 limes

Toss the diced cucumber and green tomatoes in a colander with 1½ tablespoons (24g) of the salt. Cover with a lid and let drain at room temperature for 4 to 5 hours.

Poach the carrots in a small pan of boiling water for about 2 minutes, until slightly tender. Drain and plunge into cold water, then drain again and set aside.

Once the cucumbers and tomatoes have drained, discard the liquid and rinse the vegetables under cold water. Drain thoroughly, then transfer to a deep work bowl. Add the mango, ginger, and hot peppers to the vegetables.

Heat the oil in a small sauté pan over medium-high heat and add the mustard seeds and cumin seeds. Toast the seeds until the mustard seeds begin to pop, then add to the vegetable mixture. Add the coriander, fennel seeds, mace, and star anise and stir to combine the spices thoroughly. Transfer to a large preserving pan and set aside.

In a separate saucepan, heat the vinegar, sugar, and the remaining 1 tablespoon (14g) salt. Add the tamarind pulp and stir to dissolve.

Sterilize the jar(s), lid(s), and ring(s) in a saucepan of lightly boiling water.

Add the vinegar mixture to the vegetables in the preserving pan and set over medium heat. Cook for 10 minutes, or until slightly tender (no longer crunchy), then add the prepared carrots and lime zest. Transfer to the prepared jar(s) and seal (see page 17). Store in a cool, dark place for up to 1 year. Refrigerate after opening.

Blood Peach Chutney

The blood peach is an unusual Old World variety that became popular with Native Americans, as it could be grown easily from seed. Its use has given rise to its other popular name, the Indian blood peach. The peach is a clingstone variety with dark crimson skin and flesh. Because of its distinctive tart flavor and firmness, the blood peach is ideal for canning and for chutneys. Lacking access to blood peaches, choose an under-ripe clingstone variety or look for flat or donut peaches, also called Saturn peaches.

Yield: 1 quart (1 liter)

2½ pounds (1.25kg) firm, under-ripe blood peaches

¼ cup (60ml) almond or virgin (cold-pressed) sesame oil

1 tablespoon (10g) black mustard seeds

1 cup (250g) organic sugar

¾ cup (180ml) red wine vinegar

1½ tablespoons (40g) freshly grated ginger

1 medium red onion (about 8 ounces/250g), cut in half lengthwise, then very thinly sliced

2 tablespoons (10g) Korean chile flakes (*gochugaru*), or to taste

1 teaspoon ground star anise

1 teaspoon ground cardamom

1 tablespoon (15g) kosher sea salt

Grated zest of 1 lime

Wash the peaches and score the bottom of each fruit with an X. Bring a large pot of water to a full rolling boil, then reduce the heat to a steady simmer. While the water is heating, fill a large work bowl with ice water and ice cubes. Place the scored peaches in the hot water and poach for about 40 seconds. Remove from the hot water and immediately plunge the poached peaches into the ice water. Starting at the X, peel away the skins, then cut the peaches in half and remove the pits. Cut the peaches into large dice and set aside.

Heat the oil in a small saucepan over high heat until quivering. Add the mustard seeds and toast until they begin to crackle and pop. Remove the saucepan from the heat and set aside to cool.

Combine the sugar and vinegar in a large nonreactive preserving pan and bring to a full boil over medium-high heat. Cook for about 5 minutes, until the mixture turns syrupy, then add the diced peaches, ginger, onion, Korean chile flakes, star anise, cardamom, and salt. Reduce the heat to medium and simmer, stirring from time to time, until the peaches are tender but not soft, 25 to 30 minutes.

Sterilize the jar(s), lid(s), and ring(s) in a large pot of lightly boiling water.

Stir in the cooled oil and mustard seeds and the lime zest and cook for 3 more minutes. Transfer to the prepared jar(s) and seal (see page 17). Store in a cool, dark place; this chutney is best used within 6 months.

Chilean *Pebre*

Pebre is the national salsa of Chile. There are hundreds of heirloom recipes, but all of them share the common feature of a soupy texture, as this salsa is eaten as a dip. The pepper of choice is *merkén*, a powder made from smoked *aji cacho de cabra* (goat's horn pepper), first cultivated by the Mapuche peoples of Chile. The green pepper of choice is pale white-green *aji cristal*, which adds crisp, celery-like texture, but any sweet green pepper can be substituted.

Traditionally, *pebre* is prepared and served fresh, but this recipe allows you to seal it in jars for storage. When you are ready to serve, just refresh it with a little lime juice and adjust the seasonings. If you opt to serve it fresh, the flavor actually improves when the salsa is covered and refrigerated overnight. And leftover *pebre* makes an extraordinary addition to meatloaf.

Yield: 1½ pints (750ml)

2½ cups (375g) minced mild onion

2 large garlic cloves, minced

1⅔ cups (275g) minced red bell pepper

½ cup (125g) minced *aji cristal*, or other sweet green peppers

2 teaspoons *merkén* or chipotle pepper powder, or to taste

½ cup (25g) finely minced cilantro leaves

⅔ cup (160ml) olive oil

5 tablespoons (75ml) fresh lime juice

3 tablespoons (45ml) white wine vinegar

1 tablespoon (5g) crumbled dried oregano

1 tablespoon (5g) ground cumin

Salt and freshly ground pepper

Sterilize the jar(s), lid(s), and ring(s) in a large pot of lightly boiling water.

Combine all the ingredients in a large bowl, then transfer into the prepared jars. Place the jars in a glass pie plate and transfer to the microwave oven. Carefully fill the pie plate half-full with hot water. Follow the instructions for the microwave method on page 17 to seal.

Store in a cool, dark place and use within 6 months.

Blueberry Chutney

The best berries for this delicate yet spicy condiment should be whitish-green with no sign of color. Due to the high pectin content of unripe berries, this chutney will set with a texture similar to marmalade. While the recipe calls for serrano peppers, as they are generally available, you can use whatever hot green peppers you prefer. One of my friends observed cynically that this recipe is one way to beat the birds (who usually claim the best of each year's crop), but guess what? It also makes spring blueberries worth waiting for, *before* the birds!

Yield: About 2 quarts (2 liters)—I usually use seven 8-ounce (250-ml) jars

1½ pounds (750g) fresh green (unripe) blueberries

3 cups (750g) organic sugar

½ cup (125ml) white wine vinegar

1 medium onion (about 8 ounces/250g), coarsely chopped

4 garlic cloves, minced (about 2 tablespoons)

2 tablespoons (30g) freshly grated ginger

1 tablespoon (5g) curry powder

4 green serrano peppers, seeded and chopped

1½ tablespoons (25g) kosher sea salt

2 tablespoons (30ml) vegetable oil

1 tablespoon (10g) yellow mustard seeds

1 teaspoon whole cumin seeds

½ cup (50g) slivered almonds

Sterilize the jar(s), lid(s), and ring(s) in a large pot of lightly boiling water.

Pick the berries from their stems and discard any that are blemished. Combine the berries with the sugar, vinegar, onion, garlic, ginger, curry powder, serrano peppers, and salt in a nonreactive preserving pan and set over medium heat. Stew the mixture gently for 15 minutes, or until the berries are soft, then remove from the heat.

Transfer to a food processor or blender and process until reduced to smooth pulp. Wash and thoroughly dry the preserving pan.

Return the pan to the stovetop and add the oil, mustard seeds, and cumin. Toast the seeds over medium-high heat until the mustard seeds begin to pop, then reduce the heat and carefully add the pureed berry mixture, taking care that it does not splatter. Stir well and bring the batter to a gentle boil, then add the almonds and continue to boil for at least 3 and up to 5 minutes. Transfer to the prepared jar(s) and seal (see page 17). Store in a cool, dark place for up to 2 years.

Green Tomato Chutney with Nigella

One of the delightful features of this Indian-style chutney is the addition of toasted nigella seeds. *Nigella sativa*, called *kalonji* in India, is also known as *gith* in old English herbals. It is sometimes sold as "onion seed" because that is what it resembles both in appearance and taste. Toasting the spices is important in this recipe because it adds a rich nutty flavor. You can also add toasted unsalted pistachios during the last twenty-five minutes of cooking. Do not hold back on the hot peppers—this recipe is better when it is spicy.

Yield: About 2 quarts (2 liters)

¼ cup (60ml) virgin (cold-pressed) sesame oil

2 teaspoons nigella seeds

1 teaspoon whole Lucknow fennel seeds

1 teaspoon whole cumin seeds

1 teaspoon white mustard seeds

3 tablespoons (35g) minced hot red peppers, or to taste

1½ cups (375ml) white wine vinegar

2 cups (500g) organic sugar

6 garlic cloves, minced

2¼ pounds (about 1kg) green tomatoes, finely diced

4 cups (500g) finely diced onion

3 tablespoons (45g) kosher sea salt, or to taste (depending on the acidity of the tomatoes)

1 tablespoon (5g) ground coriander

Sterilize the jar(s), lid(s), and ring(s) in a large pot of lightly boiling water.

In a large nonreactive preserving pan, heat the oil over medium-high heat and add the nigella, fennel, cumin, and mustard seeds and the hot peppers. Cook uncovered for 2 minutes, or until the mustard seeds begin to pop.

Add the vinegar and sugar, then reduce the heat and simmer until the sugar is completely dissolved and turns thick and syrupy, about 5 minutes.

Stir in the garlic, tomatoes, onion, salt, and coriander, increase the heat to medium-high, and cook, stirring frequently, until the mixture thickens, about 25 minutes, Adjust the seasonings, then transfer to the prepared jar(s) and seal (see page 17). Store in a cool, dark place for up to 2 years. Refrigerate after opening.

Hot Pepper Rings with Huacatay and Lime

This South American–style pickle cashes in on the unique flavor of the popular Andean herb known as *huacatay*, or black mint. It is not a true mint but rather a relative of the marigold. The herb is easy to grow and seeds are available online from several specialty seed companies (see Sources, page 199). For more on *huacatay*, refer to *Aji de Huacatay* (page 50). While there is no immediate substitute for the distinct flavor of *huacatay*, you can approximate it here by mixing equal parts tarragon, cilantro, and spearmint (5 grams each).

Yield: 1 quart (1 liter)

1 pound (500g) sliced sweet peppers (mixed colors), seeds removed

8 ounces (250g) sliced hot red peppers (such as a mix of Roughwood Fairy Horns and *ajis charapita rojo*), seeds removed

4 ounces (125g) sliced green jalapeño peppers, seeds removed

1 medium onion (about 8 ounces/250g), cut in half lengthwise, then thinly sliced

4 large garlic cloves, sliced in half lengthwise

24 whole allspice berries

1 large bunch (25g) cilantro (leaves only)

1 medium bunch (½ ounce/15g) *huacatay* leaves, stripped from stems

Grated zest of 1 lime

¾ cup (180ml) white wine vinegar

3 tablespoons (45g) kosher sea salt

½ cup (125g) organic sugar

Sterilize the jar(s), lid(s), and ring(s) in a large pot of lightly boiling water.

Mix the sliced sweet and hot peppers, the onion, garlic, allspice berries, cilantro, *huacatay*, and lime zest in a large bowl until combined. Transfer the mixture to the prepared jar(s) and pack the contents tightly with a wooden mallet.

In a medium saucepan, combine 3 cups (750ml) spring water, the vinegar, salt, and sugar and bring to a rolling boil over high heat. Cook for 3 minutes, then pour the hot brine over the pepper mixture and seal (see page 17). Store in a cool, dark place for up to 1 year. Refrigerate after opening.

Madras-Style Hot Shallot Chutney

This spicy onion celebration is excellent with grilled or fried fish. Be sure the mustard seeds are fresh so they add the best nutty flavor to the chutney.

Yield: 1 quart (1 liter)

2 pounds (1kg) trimmed and peeled shallots (weight after trimming and peeling)

1-pound (500g) onions, quartered lengthwise, then cut in half again

½ cup (90g) minced hot peppers, or more to taste

1½ cups (375g) tomato paste

1 cup (250ml) red wine vinegar

¼ cup (60g) organic sugar

2 tablespoons (30g) kosher sea salt

1 tablespoon (5g) ground cumin

1 tablespoon (5g) ground coriander

1 tablespoon (5g) ground turmeric

½ cup (125ml) virgin (cold-pressed) sesame oil

2 tablespoons (20g) black mustard seeds

Grated zest of 2 lemons

Sterilize the jar(s), lid(s), and ring(s) in a large pot of lightly boiling water.

Cut the shallots in half or quarters depending on size; if especially small, leave them whole. The object is to have the shallot and onion wedges more or less the same size. Combine the shallots, onions, and minced hot peppers in a large bowl and set aside. In a medium bowl, combine the tomato paste, vinegar, 1 cup (250ml) spring water, the sugar, salt, cumin, coriander, and turmeric and set aside.

In a deep nonreactive preserving pan, heat the oil over medium-high heat. Once hot, add the mustard seeds and toast until they begin to pop continuously and smell nutty, 2 to 3 minutes.

Add the reserved shallot mixture, cover, and cook, stirring occasionally to keep the onions from scorching on the bottom or getting too soft, about 4 minutes. Reduce the heat to medium and stir in the tomato paste mixture. Cook uncovered until thick and the onions are tender, another 15 to 20 minutes.

Remove from the heat, add the lemon zest, then transfer to the prepared jars and seal (see page 17). Store in a cool, dark place for up to 1 year. Refrigerate after opening.

Pepper Chutney with Curry

This chutney cooks rosy-orange from the tamarind, so the color of your peppers is not critical, although red peppers will make it somewhat darker. Tamarind also acts as a thickener because of its high pectin, so this chutney has a jamlike consistency. Two words of caution: Because it is heavy and thick, this chutney may scorch in the preserving pan—keep an eye on it and be ready to stir. It may also jam a food processor or blender if too much is pureed at once. As a condiment, it is excellent with lamb and grilled meat or with grilled vegetables. You may add 1 tablespoon (15ml) virgin sesame oil to the top of each jar of chutney prior to sealing them.

Yield: 2½ pints (1.25 liters)

8 ounces (250g) sweet peppers, seeded and sliced

8 ounces (250g) hot peppers, seeded and sliced

1 mango (about 2 pounds/1kg), peeled, pitted, and chopped

6 garlic cloves, chopped

5 tablespoons (4 ounces/125g) tamarind pulp (picked of seeds or seed fragments)

1½ tablespoons (25g) kosher sea salt

2 to 3 tablespoons (10 to 15g) curry powder (depending on freshness)

1½ cups (375ml) distilled white vinegar

1 cup (250g) organic sugar

½ cup (125ml) fresh lime juice

Sterilize the jar(s), lid(s), and ring(s) in a large pot of lightly boiling water.

Combine all of the ingredients except the lime juice in a deep nonreactive preserving pan and heat over medium heat, stirring well to dissolve the tamarind pulp. Then cover and simmer until the ingredients are thoroughly soft and nearly falling apart, about 20 minutes, stirring from time to time to prevent scorching. Working in batches, transfer the mixture to a food processor or blender and process until smooth and creamy. Transfer the mixture to a clean preserving pan. Reheat for 5 minutes, then stir in the lime juice. Transfer to the prepared jar(s) and seal (see page 17). Store in a cool, dark place for up to 2 years. Refrigerate after opening.

Cilantro Chutney

Commercial cilantro chutney (commonly labeled coriander chutney) can be found in most Indian markets, but in order to produce it, the chutney must be processed and canned like tomato sauce. Cooking it muddies the color and degrades the fresh, complex flavors, which is why there are so many additives in commercial brands. While my recipe will submit to canning like any sauce or pesto by simply bringing it to a boil and then sealing it in hot jars, I personally think a much better plan of action is to freeze it. The fresh flavor is better preserved, and the color does not fade. All the same, do not store the frozen chutney for more than six months, as even frozen foods degrade over time.

The amount of sugar is a matter of taste—¼ cup (60g) yields a tart flavor, while ½ cup (125g) changes the result to sweet and sour. Hot peppers, however, are a must and should be green; otherwise they will discolor the chutney.

Yield: About 3½ cups (875ml)

6 ounces (150g) hot green peppers (or green jalapeños), or more to taste, stemmed and seeded

1 cup (75g) shredded unsweetened (raw) coconut

¾ cup (180ml) virgin (cold-pressed) sesame oil

4 garlic cloves, minced

1 cup (250ml) distilled white vinegar

½ cup (125g) organic sugar, or to taste

1 tablespoon (15g) kosher sea salt, plus more to taste

1 tablespoon (5g) ground coriander

2 tablespoons (10g) ground ginger

3 cups (75g) cilantro leaves, rinsed well

Coarsely chop the peppers and put them in a food processor or blender along with the coconut, oil, garlic, vinegar, sugar, salt, coriander, and ginger. Process until the mixture forms a thick batter, 1 to 2 minutes.

Add the cilantro and process until reduced to a pulp. Adjust the seasonings (you may need as much as an additional 2 teaspoons salt, depending on taste). Serve immediately or pour into sterilized quilted preserve jar(s), cover with screw top lid(s), and freeze for up to 6 months.

Jamaican-Style Chutney for Barbecue

By *barbecue*, I am referring to meat (generally goat) spit-roasted over an open flame. That at least is the original Jamaican context for this old-time recipe. Years ago, when I purchased the loose ends of the Margaret Cook collection, hidden among her unsung culinary treasures was an 1897 cookbook from Jamaica, where I found one of the best recipes typifying the Caribbean penchant for blending hot, spicy, and in this case, sweet. I have taken that recipe (one of my favorites) and reinvented it here. This chutney can be made as spicy as you prefer and will improve in flavor if allowed to mellow for at least one month before using. You can serve it simply alongside barbecue as a side or strain out the fruit beforehand and apply the liquid to the meat while it grills—then mix the reserved fruit with chopped fresh pineapple to serve as a relish. Try it, too, as a basting sauce for grilled pumpkin or fish. Since the chutney is pretty potent, put it up in small jelly jars.

Yield: About 9 cups (2.25 liters)

3½ pounds (750g) pared and pitted fresh slightly green mango (weight after paring and pitting)

8 ounces (250g) seedless green raisins

2 medium onions (about 1 pound/500g), cut in half lengthwise, then thinly sliced

½ cup (125g) freshly grated ginger

¼ cup (60g) very finely minced garlic (or use a garlic press)

Grated zest and juice of 1 lime

1 tablespoon (5g) grated bitter orange zest

½ cup (125ml) freshly squeezed bitter orange juice

¼ cup (60ml) tomato paste

1 tablespoon (5g) powdered annatto (achiote)

3 cups (750ml) red wine vinegar

1½ cups (250g) organic muscovado sugar or dark brown sugar

¼ cup (60g) kosher sea salt

Cayenne pepper or other ground hot pepper of your choice, optional

Sterilize the jar(s), lid(s), and ring(s) in a large pot of lightly boiling water.

Chop the mango into small irregular pieces. Combine with the raisins, onions, ginger, garlic, lime zest and juice, bitter orange zest and juice, tomato paste, annatto, vinegar, sugar, and salt in a large nonreactive preserving pan. Stew over a medium-low heat until the mango begins to break down, 15 to 20 minutes. Adjust the seasonings and add hot pepper to taste, if using.

Transfer to prepared jars and seal (see page 17). Allow the chutney to mellow a month or two in a cool, dark place before using. Store in a cool, dark place for up to 2 years. Refrigerate after opening.

Pepper Sherry
(Borie's Scotch Bonnet Sherry)

Pepper sherry was once a Philadelphia institution, a necessary condiment for elegant soups, terrapin dishes, and seafood in general. No well-appointed table was without it. The most sought-after label was Borie's, and until 1988 it was still made by John Wagner and Sons, Inc., an old Philadelphia firm specializing in fine teas, wines, and spices. The Borie recipe traces to Elizabeth Beauveau, who with her five daughters escaped an 1802 slave rebellion in Haiti and soon thereafter set up a boarding house in Philadelphia catering to French immigrants. From Cap Francois, Madame Beauveau brought seeds for the distinctive pepper that the family had used for making the pepper sherry they had been exporting to Philadelphia since the 1780s—the same variety today known as the orange Scotch bonnet pepper.

Madame Beauveau's pepper sherry tradition was carried forward by her daughter, Sophie Beauveau, who married J. J. Borie in 1808 and continued to grow the peppers in a greenhouse at their Eaglesfield Farm, in what is now the Fairmount Park section of Philadelphia. Those peppers supplied the family with the ingredients for their famed pepper sherry, a basic condiment for classic Philadelphia pepper pot soup.

Yield: 1 quart (1 liter)

4 ounces (65g) ripe orange Scotch bonnet peppers, stemmed and seeded

2 large garlic cloves, crushed

4 fresh bay leaves, bruised

6 whole allspice berries

1 quart (1 liter) Madeira or sweet sherry, or more as needed

Sterilize the jar(s), lid(s), and ring(s), or bottle(s) in a large pot of lightly boiling water, then wipe them dry. Once the bottles or jars are cool, add the prepared peppers, garlic, bay leaves, and allspice, dividing them evenly. Cover with the Madeira, then seal tightly. No cooking is required.

Set the sealed jar(s) or bottle(s) away in a cool, dark place for 1 month to mature. After the infusion has cured, strain out the peppers, garlic, bay leaves, and allspice, wash out the bottle, then pour the pepper sherry back into the same bottle and store in a cool place out of direct sunlight until needed.

Since this recipe makes a concentrated pepper sherry, the strength of the spices can be adjusted by diluting the finished product with more Madeira according to taste.

Pepper Vinegar (Hot Pepper Sauce)

This classic Pennsylvania Dutch recipe traces back to *Die Geschickte Hausfrau* (The Handy Housewife) of 1848 but has undergone many changes and adjustments since then. It is used like catsup on fried oysters, shellfish, or whatever dish may call for hot sauce. The amount of hot peppers you put in is a matter of personal taste, yet two points remain fairly consistent: Be certain all pepper seeds are removed before you puree the peppers (the seeds are bitter and unsightly), and the final texture of the sauce should resemble a thick, creamy batter.

Yield: 9 cups (2.25 liters)

1½ pounds (750g) stemmed and seeded red bell peppers (weight after stemming and seeding), chopped

8 ounces (250g) stemmed and seeded hot cayenne type-peppers (weight after stemming and seeding), chopped

1 medium onion (about 8 ounces/250g), thinly sliced

3 cups (750ml) white wine vinegar

2 cups (500ml) Garlic Vinegar (page 194)

⅔ cup (155g) organic sugar

1½ tablespoons (25g) kosher sea salt

Sterilize the jar(s), lid(s), and ring(s), or bottle(s) in a large pot of lightly boiling water and wipe dry.

Combine the peppers, onion, and white wine vinegar in a food processor or high-speed blender and process until it forms a thick, coarse batter, 1 to 2 minutes.

Transfer to a large nonreactive preserving pan and add the garlic vinegar, sugar, and salt. Bring the batter to a simmer over medium-high heat and cook until thickened, about 20 minutes. Transfer the hot batter back to the food processor or blender and process again to break it down into a thick, creamy consistency.

Transfer the batter back to the preserving pan and return to a simmer over medium-high heat. Once boiling hot, pour into the prepared jar(s) and top with the lids and rings, then turn upside-down to cool (because the mixture is boiling hot already, there's no need to use the microwave to seal). Store in a cool dry closet for up to 3 years. Refrigerate after opening.

Pickled Martynias with Burr Gherkins and Cumari Peppers

Martynias, or devil's claws, have been common in early American kitchen gardens since the 1840s. The young green pods can be used exactly like okra and can also be pickled, as according to this Brazilian recipe. But first a word about Cumari peppers, which give this pickle its heat and special character.

Cumari peppers are wild peppers from the Cumari region of Brazil. The name is applied to several types of indigenous peppers, although the Cumari Pollux (which is a distinct species of its own) is often considered the truest example of this type. However, Cumari Pollux is not easy to come by, while the small, yellow berry-shaped Cumari do Para (*Capsicum chinense*), a relative of the habanero, is now generally available in the States. Their intensely hot, smoky flavor is unique and much appreciated in Brazilian cuisine. If you cannot locate Cumari peppers, use chopped habaneros according to your taste; if you do not like hot peppers, simply leave them out. I prefer Cumari do Para to other Cumari peppers for its ornamental appearance and because its flavor is both sweet and hot. For comments about burr gherkins, see page 168.

Yield: 2 pints (1 liter)

12 ounces (375g) small, tender martynia pods or a mix of martynia pods and baby okra

4 ounces (125g) small burr gherkins, trimmed of stems, or freshly picked French cornichons

1 tablespoon (15g) kosher sea salt, plus more for boiling

2 garlic cloves, thinly sliced lengthwise

4 fresh bay leaves

½ medium onion (about 4 ounces/125g), thinly sliced

8 whole allspice berries

16 Cumari peppers (10g), stemmed and slit in half lengthwise

⅓ cup (25g) sliced sweet red peppers

3 cups (750ml) white wine vinegar

¼ cup (60g) organic sugar

Sterilize 2 jars, lids, and rings in a large pot of lightly boiling water.

Trim the martynias of their stems and tips (also trim the baby okra or cornichons, if using). Weigh the vegetables, keeping the martynias separate, to be certain you have a total of 1 pound (500g), then set aside.

Bring another pan of lightly salted water to a full rolling boil over medium-high heat. Reduce the heat so that the water is barely quivering, then add the martynias and poach for 5 minutes. Drain and combine with the other vegetables in a deep work bowl.

Add the garlic, bay leaves, and onion. Put 4 whole allspice berries in each of the prepared jars, then pack the jars with the vegetable mixture, making certain that each jar receives 2 bay leaves. Top each jar with 8 Cumari peppers.

Combine the vinegar, ½ cup (125ml) spring water, the sugar, and salt in a small nonreactive preserving pan and bring to a rolling boil over medium-high heat. Boil for 3 minutes, then pour over the vegetables and seal (see page 17). Store in a cool, dark place for up to 2 years. Refrigerate after opening.

Pickled Okra with Chipotle Pepper

This is a great side dish with grilled meats or barbecue or cheese and cold beer. You can add whole chipotle peppers, or pods broken into pieces, to give the pickle more spicy heat. For eye appeal and a subtle difference in textures, I like to mix different varieties of okra, especially Stubby (which is small) and White Velvet.

Yield: 1½ quarts (1.5 liters)

2 pounds (1kg) freshly harvested okra, stems trimmed off

4 garlic cloves, cut lengthwise into thin slices

6 fresh bay leaves

½ medium onion (about 4 ounces/125g), thinly sliced

1 teaspoon whole allspice berries (about 30 berries)

1½ quarts (1.5 liters) white wine vinegar

1 cup (250g) organic sugar

2 tablespoons (30g) kosher sea salt

¼ cup (60ml tomato paste

3 tablespoons (15g) ground chipotle pepper

Sterilize the jar(s), lid(s), and ring(s) in a large pot of lightly boiling water.

Combine the okra, garlic, bay leaves, onion, and allspice berries in a deep work bowl and mix well, then pack the mixture tightly into the prepared jar(s).

Combine the vinegar, 1½ cups (375ml) spring water, the sugar, salt, tomato paste, and chipotle pepper in a large nonreactive preserving pan, whisking to dissolve the tomato paste, and bring to a rolling boil over high heat. Boil for 3 minutes, then pour over the okra mixture and seal (see page 17). Store in a cool, dark place for up to 2 years, but this pickle is best when used within 9 months, since its flavors will begin to fade. Refrigerate after opening.

Stuffed Baby Peppers

The peppers of choice for this recipe are miniature sweet peppers one to two inches in diameter and only about one inch thick—they resemble little pattypan squash in shape. My two favorite varieties, both of which are thick, sweet, and crunchy, are Weaver's Mennonite stuffing pepper and Mammi Huber's stuffing pepper. Weaver's can be traced back to my great-great grandfather, Abraham Weaver, who is thought to have brought back Hungarian seeds from the Paris Exposition in 1878. Mammi Huber's is a newer variety from an old-order Mennonite vendor in Hinkletown, Pennsylvania. Today seeds for both varieties are available from the Roughwood Seed Collection (see Sources, page 199).

Yield: 1 quart (1 liter)

1-pound (500g) baby sweet peppers (about 14 to 15; see headnote)

2 tablespoons (30g) kosher sea salt

1 cup (125g) finely shredded cabbage

1 tablespoon (25g) freshly grated horseradish

1 tablespoon (25g) freshly grated ginger

1½ teaspoons yellow mustard seeds

2 teaspoons ground coriander

1 teaspoon whole celery seeds

1 to 2 teaspoons ground hot pepper (Indian or Korean recommended), or to taste

3 ounces (90g) pearl onions (about 6), peeled and halved lengthwise

6 garlic cloves, halved lengthwise

4 fresh bay leaves

1½ cups (375g) organic sugar

1½ cups (375ml) white wine vinegar

1 tablespoon (15g) kosher sea salt

Sterilize the jar(s), lid(s), and ring(s) in a large pot of lightly boiling water.

Wash the peppers thoroughly, then cut away the stem parts, removing the lids in the same manner as carving a pumpkin into a jack-o-lantern, and reserve the lids in an airtight container in the refrigerator overnight. Carefully remove the seeds from the lidded peppers with a spoon, leaving them otherwise intact.

Transfer the peppers to a deep glass or ceramic bowl and dissolve the salt in 1 quart (1 liter) of spring water in a separate bowl. Pour the brine over the peppers and let stand uncovered at room temperature overnight. The next day, drain and discard the brine, but do not rinse the peppers. Chop the reserved pepper lids into a fine dice—you should have about ¼ cup (30g) diced peppers—and set aside.

In a large work bowl, combine the cabbage, horseradish, ginger, mustard seeds, coriander, celery seeds, ground hot pepper, and diced sweet pepper lids, and mix well.

Pressing carefully but firmly with your thumb, stuff the mixture into each pepper, then arrange the stuffed peppers three to a layer in the prepared jars (being certain to keep them lidded-side up). Fit the pearl onions, garlic, and bay leaves into spaces between the peppers.

Once the jar(s) are full, combine the sugar, vinegar, and salt in a medium saucepan. Place over medium-high heat, bring just to a rolling boil, and reduce the liqued for 5 minutes. Pour the hot brine over the peppers and seal (see page 17). Store the jar(s) upright so the stuffing remains inside the peppers. Keep for 2 to 3 years in a cool, dark place. Refrigerate after opening.

Pickled Mouse Melons

Mouse melons (*Melothria scabra*) are a climbing vine from Mexico and Central America. The tiny fruits resemble miniature watermelons and can be eaten raw or cooked. In pickles, they are bit like mini cucumbers, but are best sliced in half; otherwise, the skins can be tough, especially on mature fruit. Be sure to put cilantro leaves on the bottom of the jar before filling it and another bunch on top. That boost of flavor is essential!

Yield: 1½ quarts (1.5 liters)

1 pound 4 ounces (625g) young mouse melons
(try to find ones about 1 inch/2.5cm long)

4 ounces (125g) pearl onions or small shallots, peeled

6 fresh bay leaves

2 large garlic cloves, cut lengthwise into 3 or 4 slices

½ medium onion (about 4 ounces/125g), thinly sliced

1 medium sweet red pepper (about 8 ounces/250g),
cut into thin strips

2 tablespoons (30g) small-diced hot red or yellow pepper,
optional

1 tablespoon (10g) yellow mustard seeds

1 tablespoon (5g) whole coriander seeds

1 tablespoon (10g) whole black peppercorns

Leaves from 1 large bunch cilantro, divided

1½ cups (375ml) distilled white vinegar

2 tablespoons (30g) kosher sea salt

¼ cup (60g) organic sugar

Sterilize the jar(s), lid(s), and ring(s) in a large pot of lightly boiling water.

Wash and stem the mouse melons, then put them in a deep work bowl with the pearl onions, bay leaves, garlic, onion, sweet and hot peppers, mustard seeds, coriander seeds, and black peppercorns. Place half the cilantro leaves on the bottom of each prepared jar(s), then add the vegetable and herb mixture.

Heat the vinegar, 2½ cups (625ml) spring water, the salt, and sugar in a medium saucepan until hot, then pour over the vegetables. Add the remaining cilantro to top of each jar and seal (see page 17).

Let stand for 2 weeks in the refrigerator before opening. The pickle will keep for up to 1 year but is best when used within 6 months.

Sindhi-Style Mango Chutney

This is one of my all-time favorite Indian-style chutney recipes, but over the years I have tweaked it to suit my tastes by emphasizing the fruitiness and reducing some of the sharp spices and salt. To some extent, the yield will depend on the type of mango used, since some cook thicker than others. When shopping for mangoes, be certain the fruit is firm and barely half ripe—the greener the better.

Yield: 2¼ quarts (2.25 liters)—I usually use six 12-ounce (375-ml) preserve jars

12 pitted dates (3 ounces/90g), diced

4 pounds (2kg) underripe mangoes, peeled, pitted, and sliced into thin strips

1½ teaspoons finely minced hot pepper, or more to taste

½ cup (50g) sliced blanched almonds

½ cup (50g) unsalted pistachios, toasted and sliced in half or coarsely chopped

About 2 garlic cloves, cut into 25 paper-thin lengthwise slices

1 tablespoon (5g) ground cumin

½ teaspoon whole cumin seeds

1 tablespoon (5g) whole cardamom seeds (removed from pods)

2 teaspoons ground cardamom

2 teaspoons ground coriander

2 teaspoons ground cinnamon

1 teaspoon ground cloves

3 cups (750g) organic sugar

2 tablespoons (30g) kosher sea salt

1 cup (250ml) white wine vinegar

Sterilize the jar(s), lid(s), and ring(s) in a large pot of lightly boiling water.

If your dates are dry, rehydrate them by soaking them in warm water for 20 minutes, or until soft, then drain and discard the water. Combine the dates, mangoes, and hot pepper in a large work bowl. In a separate bowl, combine the almonds, pistachios, garlic, and whole and ground spices and set aside.

In a large preserving pan, combine the sugar with 1 cup (250ml) spring water and bring to a boil over medium heat; boil until the sugar has thoroughly dissolved and the mixture forms a thick syrup, about 10 minutes. Add the mango mixture and the salt and cook over medium-high heat until the mixture thickens and is reduced by about half, about 30 minutes. Add the almond mixture and the vinegar and cook for another 5 minutes.

Transfer to the prepared jar(s) and seal (see page 17). This recipe keeps well for up to 3 years in a cool, dark place. Refrigerate after opening.

Salsa Picante de Aji Dulce

Aji dulce is a relative of the habanero pepper that hails from northern South America, in particular Venezuela. The pepper ranges from heatless to mildly hot depending on the strain. Don't use less than 8 ounces (250g) of *aji dulce* or the unique flavor of this pepper will not come through. You can even increase the quantity up to 12 ounces (375g) by reducing the sweet red peppers accordingly

Yield: 3½ cups (875ml)

8 ounces (250g) chopped *aji dulce*
(weight after seeds removed)

8 ounces (250g) chopped sweet red peppers
(weight after seeds removed)

1¾ cups (430ml) white wine vinegar

⅔ cup (160ml) Garlic Vinegar (page XX)

½ cup (125g) organic sugar

1 tablespoon (15g) kosher sea salt, or to taste

Sterilize the jar(s), lid(s), and ring(s) in a large pot of lightly boiling water.

Combine the chopped peppers in a large nonreactive preserving pan with the vinegars, sugar, and salt. Cook over medium-high heat until the peppers are soft, about 15 minutes.

Remove from the heat and transfer to a food processor or high-speed blender. Process to a thick batter. Pour the batter back into the preserving pan and cook over medium heat for about 10 minutes, until thickened, then transfer to the prepared jar(s) and seal (see page 17). Keep for 1 to 2 years in a cool, dark place. Refrigerate after opening.

Salsa de Aji Amarillo with Asian Pear and Madeira

Salsas made with *aji amarillo*, one of the classic heirloom peppers handed down from the Incas and an important foundation ingredient in the traditional cuisine of the Andes, are available over the Internet, many from Peru, where this remarkable pepper originates. When dried, it is called *aji amarillo mirasol*. I think it is best when freshly harvested, as that is when its flavors are most complex. Bright golden yellow when fully ripe and fruity with subtle heat and overtones of apricot—this is one of those unusual peppers that mellows when cooked, and if kept too long in the canning jars, its spicy heat will fade away. If you prefer a smokier finish to the salsa, reduce the quantity of *ajis amarillo* and increase the amount of Scotch bonnets. This salsa is excellent with shellfish, in particular conch and scallops. Like all recipes using hot peppers, this one should be guided by your palate and comfort with spice.

I have been growing this pepper for many years from seeds given to me by the late Dr. Jean Andrews, better known as the Pepper Lady, and author of several books on peppers, who brought back a treasure trove of rare seeds from Arequipa, Peru. Thanks to her, it's now possible to grow *ajis amarillo* from seeds obtained from the Roughwood Seed Collection and Sow True Seed (see Sources, page 199). Otherwise, substitute any yellow cayenne or other hot pepper, but keep in mind that the heat will be more intense, so adjust the amount accordingly.

Yield: About 1¾ quarts (1.75 liters)—I usually use seven 8-ounce (250-ml) jars

1 pound (500g) *aji amarillo* (or yellow hot peppers of your choice)

1 tablespoon (10g) minced orange Scotch bonnet pepper or habanero pepper, or to taste

1 pound (500g) pared and cored Asian pears (weight after paring and coring; about 2 pears)

3½ cups (875ml) white wine vinegar

⅔ cup (155g) organic sugar, or more to taste

2 to 3 teaspoons kosher sea salt, or more to taste

8 fresh bay leaves

1 tablespoon (5g) grated orange zest

¾ cup (180ml) Madeira

Sterilize the jar(s), lid(s), and ring(s) in a large pot of lightly boiling water.

Seed and chop the *aji amarillos*. Combine them with the Scotch bonnet pepper, pears, vinegar, sugar, salt, and bay leaves in a large nonreactive preserving pan. Place over medium-high heat, cover, and cook until the peppers are soft, about 20 minutes.

Remove from the heat and discard the bay leaves, then transfer to a food processor or high-speed blender and process until pureed into a chunky batter, 1 to 2 minutes. Add the orange zest and process again until thick and smooth.

Rinse the preserving pan, then return the batter to the pan and cook over medium heat until thickened, about 10 minutes. Adjust the seasonings with more sugar or salt, as needed, then add the Madeira. Transfer to the prepared jar(s) and seal (see page 17). This recipe will keep for as long as 2 years, but is best used within 6 to 8 months because the heat from the peppers will fade—a characteristic of this variety. Refrigerate after opening.

Salsa de Aji Limó (Lima Pepper Salsa)

Aji limó is another Andean pepper with a distinctive flavor and color, in this case bright lemon yellow. The pods are short, flat, and tapered, with a citrus-like flavor. The intense heat mellows as the peppers cook. This recipe was inspired by a Peruvian export I found in France under the name *sauce douce aux piments*. After tinkering with it, I soon figured out that combining mangoes, peppers, mustard, and lime zest could recreate the salsa's sensational complex flavors.

Yield: 2 quarts (2 liters)

4 ounces (125g) aji limó, seeded and chopped (wear rubber gloves)

8 ounces (250g) sweet yellow or orange peppers, seeded and chopped

2 mangoes, peeled, pitted, and chopped (roughly 2 pounds/1kg whole fruit)

1 cup (250g) organic sugar

1½ tablespoons (25g) kosher sea salt

2 teaspoons ground ginger

3 tablespoons (45ml) Dijon mustard

1½ cups (375ml) Shallot Vinegar (page 194)

½ cup (35g) grated key lime zest (from about 6 limes)

Sterilize the jar(s), lid(s), and ring(s) in a large pot of lightly boiling water.

Combine the hot and sweet peppers, the mangoes, sugar, salt, ginger, mustard, and vinegar in a large nonreactive preserving pan. Place over medium heat and cook until the peppers are soft, about 25 minutes. Transfer the mixture to a food processor or high-speed blender and process until smooth, 1 to 2 minutes.

Return the batter to the preserving pan. Bring to a gentle boil over medium heat, skimming off any foam. Cook for about 10 minutes to be certain the batter is boiling hot, then remove from the heat and add the lime zest.

Transfer the salsa to the prepared jars and seal (see page 17). This will keep in a cool, dark place for up to 2 years, but is best used within 9 months, before the fruity heat from this pepper begins to fade. Refrigerate after opening.

Salsa Roja Piquante (Spicy Red Salsa)

This rich, fruity salsa promises excellent flavor with laid-back heat. The combination I prefer is half Chilean *ajis cacho de cabra* and half Nicaraguan sweet *chiltomas grande*, but any pairing of hot cayenne-type and sweet red pepper will work as long as you respect the proportions. Only pepper varieties with similar characteristics make good substitutes, otherwise the balance of flavors will be off and the salsa will turn out much hotter than intended—unless, of course, you want it that way. Mildly hot *aji cacho de cabra*, which is normally smoked by the indigenous peoples of Chile, tends to mellow a bit during cooking, which here is a plus because the heat then becomes more subtle. The best rule of thumb is to taste as you cook—if the salsa is not spicy enough, you can always add more hot pepper. Before transferring the pureed salsa into sterilized jars, you can add a variety of other ingredients, such as chopped nuts (I like pistachios), additional hot pepper, or grated lime zest for nice additional texture and flavor.

Yield: 1 to 1¼ quarts (1 to 1.25 liters)

¼ cup (60ml) olive oil

1 cup (100g) chopped onion (about ½ medium onion)

4 to 5 garlic cloves, minced

8 ounces (250g) hot red peppers, seeded and chopped

8 ounces (250g) sweet red peppers, seeded and chopped

¼ cup (60ml) tomato paste

1 tablespoon (5g) ground coriander

1 teaspoon ground cumin

½ cup (125g) clover honey

2 teaspoons kosher sea salt

1½ cups (375ml) red wine vinegar

1 cup (25g) chopped cilantro (leaves only)

Sterilize the jar(s), lid(s), and ring(s) in a large pot of lightly boiling water.

In a large nonreactive preserving pan, heat the oil over medium-high heat, then and add the onion, cover, and sweat until translucent, about 4 minutes. Add the garlic, hot and sweet peppers, tomato paste, coriander, and cumin and stir to combine.

Once the ingredients are hot, add the honey, salt, and vinegar. Cover, reduce the heat to medium, and cook until the mixture is soft and fragrant and the peppers have changed color, about 5 minutes.

Remove from the heat and transfer the mixture to a food processor or high-speed blender (wash and dry the preserving pan). Add the cilantro and process until the mixture becomes a thick, orange-colored batter, 1 to 2 minutes.

Return the batter to the clean preserving pan and put back over medium heat for 5 to 8 minutes to make certain the batter is boiling hot. Adjust the seasonings, then pour into hot sterilized jars and seal (see page 17). Keep for up to 2 years, but this recipe is best when used within 9 months. Refrigerate after opening.

Aji de Huacatay (Peruvian Peanut Salsa)

First, I should explain that *aji* is a South American term both for pepper and for a condiment, so it can mean two things at the same time if said condiment consists of peppers. That's not the case here, as *huacatay* is a species of marigold (*Tagetes minuta*) that can grow up to twelve feet (three meters) high if the soil is rich enough, with large, fernlike leaves, which some claim resemble marijuana. While the flowers are minimal, the leaves provide Andean cuisine with a unique culinary herb vaguely reminiscent of mint, hence its common name black mint. For home gardeners using this recipe, *huacatay* is easy to grow and will reseed from year to year.

Aji de huacatay is made exclusively from the herb's leaves and has been a feature of indigenous Peruvian cookery for many centuries. Today it is prepared in a variety of ways and frequently contains queso fresco, an ingredient unknown to the Incas. Those made with cheese have a thick, hummus-like texture, which is then thinned with canned milk or water. My recipe is somewhat different in that it is essentially a sour-spicy puree similar to an Indian-style cilantro chutney (page 28), inspired by *ocopa arequipeña*, a type of *aji de huacatay* peculiar to Arequipa, Peru. The distinctive ingredient here is peanut butter, which acts as a binder. Like the cilantro chutney recipe, this salsa can be cooked and put up in jars, but it is most flavorful when used fresh or frozen for later use. In Peru this salsa is normally paired with grilled meat or vegetables, fried chicken, or fried *cui* (guinea pig). You can add more *aji amarillo* if you want the salsa to be spicy. While fresh peppers will always yield the best results, you can also make this recipe with ¼ cup (60ml) jarred *aji amarillo* puree, available online.

Yield: About 3 cups (750ml)

6 ounces (150g) fresh *aji amarillo* peppers, trimmed and seeded

1 cup (250g) unsalted creamy peanut butter

¾ cup (180ml) olive oil

4 garlic cloves, minced

¾ cup (180ml) white wine vinegar

½ cup (125g) organic sugar, or more to taste

1 tablespoon (15g) kosher sea salt

1 tablespoon (5g) ground coriander

1 tablespoon (5g) crumbled dried spearmint (*yerba buena*)

3 cups (50g) fresh *huacatay* (leaves only), plus more for serving

Freshly grated lime zest, for serving

Coarsely chop the peppers and combine in a food processor or high-speed blender with the peanut butter, oil, garlic, vinegar, sugar, salt, coriander, and spearmint. Process until the mixture forms a thick batter.

Chop the *huacatay* and add it to the batter, then process until smooth. Taste and adjust the seasonings. Serve immediately or freeze for later use (see page 28). When serving, garnish with minced *huacatay* and freshly grated lime zest. Keep for up to 2 years in a cool, dark place, but this recipe is best used within 9 months. Refrigerate after opening.

Salsa Verde de Tomatillos

For inspiration for this recipe I explored a number of regional Mexican cookbooks, keeping in mind that many Americans do not care for tomatillos. I think it's the off taste sometimes apparent in the green ones sold in stateside supermarkets. Most likely they are not fresh, and after a week in transit they develop starches or acidity that demands vigorous culinary intervention. I prefer yellow tomatillos because they are sweeter and more like tomatoes in flavor, although freshly harvested green varieties will also work well here. Since tomatillos can be so variable in flavor, the amount of sugar and vinegar will vary with each batch, so treat my proportions below as suggestions. You may need to add more or less depending on the fruit you are using. Like Cilantro Chutney (page 28) and *Aji de Huacatay* (page 54), this salsa can be frozen after adding the spices rather than canning it.

Yield: 2 quarts (2 liters)

2½ pounds (1.25kg) husked yellow or green tomatillos

⅓ cup (90ml) olive oil

8 ounces (250g) chopped onions

1 pound (500g) trimmed and seeded green bell peppers (weight after trimming and seeding)

6 large garlic cloves, minced

2 tablespoons (10g) ground chipotle pepper, or more to taste

1 cup (250ml) white wine vinegar

¾ cup (185g) organic sugar

1½ tablespoons (25g) kosher sea salt

1¾ cups (45g) chopped cilantro (leaves only), plus more for serving

1½ tablespoons (8g) ground coriander

1 teaspoon ground cumin

Grated lime zest, for serving

Sterilize the jar(s), lid(s), and ring(s) in a large pot of lightly boiling water.

Chop or quarter the tomatillos (depending on desired texture; chopped ones cook more quickly) and set aside.

In a deep nonreactive preserving pan, heat the oil over medium-high heat. Add the onions, then reduce the heat to medium, cover, and sweat for 3 minutes. Add the tomatillos, bell peppers, garlic, chipotle, vinegar, sugar, and salt and stew over medium heat until the vegetables are soft and turning to pulp, about 20 minutes. Let cool in the preserving pan, then add the cilantro.

Transfer the mixture to a food processor or high-speed blender and process to a smooth batter consistency, 1 to 2 minutes. Wash and dry the preserving pan, then pour in the batter and put back over medium heat. Bring the batter to a gentle boil, add the coriander and cumin, then taste and adjust the seasonings.

Transfer to the prepared jars and when room temperature, seal the lids tightly by hand. Freeze (quilted jelly jars are best for this purpose). Add fresh lime zest and additional cilantro right before serving. Keep frozen for up to 3 years, but the salsa's flavor is best when used within 1 year.

Spicy Baby Corn and Okra with Fish Peppers

This rustic, farmhouse pickle is great for fried oyster picnics because it can be served as finger food. Since the corn and okra are left whole, I recommend using a single 1-gallon (4-liter) wide-mouthed canning jar or dividing everything between smaller jars. For eye appeal and subtle differences in texture, I like mixing different varieties of okra, especially Stubby (when small), and White and Red Velvet okra. I also use fish peppers in various stages of ripeness, from white with green stripes, to orange, and then red. The fish pepper was saved from extinction by my grandfather, who acquired seeds during the 1940s from folk painter Horace Pippin. A famous Baltimore hot sauce called Snake Oil is now made exclusively from fish pepper. Since its heat is mild, you need to use quite a few; lacking fish peppers, substitute jalapeños or hot Thai peppers according to your heat tolerance.

Yield: 3½ to 4 quarts (3.5 to 4 liters)

1 pound (500g) freshly harvested okra, stems and tips trimmed

1 pound (500g) fresh baby corn

2 medium onions (about 1 pound/250g), cut in half lengthwise, then thinly sliced

3 to 4 sweet red peppers (1½ to 2 pounds/375g to 1kg), sliced into rings

4 garlic cloves, thinly sliced

6 fresh bay leaves

3 ounces (90g) fish peppers, mixed colors (about 15 to 20; substitute jalapeños or hot Thai peppers), stem ends trimmed to expose seeds

15 whole allspice berries

1 tablespoon (10g) white mustard seeds

1 tablespoon (5g) fresh thyme leaves

1 tablespoon (10g) whole black peppercorns

1½ quarts (1.5 liters) white wine vinegar

1 cup (250g) organic sugar

Sterilize the jar(s), lid(s), and ring(s) in a large pot of lightly boiling water.

Combine the okra, corn, onions, sweet peppers, garlic, bay leaves, fish peppers, allspice, mustard seeds, thyme, and peppercorns in a large work bowl and stir to mix, then transfer to the prepared jar(s). Make certain that the ingredients are evenly distributed.

Combine the vinegar, 1½ cups (375ml) spring water, the sugar, and salt in a large nonreactive preserving pan. Bring to a boil over medium-high heat and cook for 3 minutes. Pour this over the vegetable mixture and seal (see page 17)—if you prefer to use a water bath, allow at least 20 minutes. Even without a water bath, this pickle is fairly stable if stored in a cool, dark place and will keep for up to 2 years; however, it is best used within 9 months.

Spicy Cauliflower and Broccoli Pickle

This pickle's heat is what recommends it especially as a cold-weather side dish, but it depends entirely on the choice of peppers. If you prefer even more heat, slice the peppers halfway to the stems and leave the seeds in. For this recipe I used fish peppers, as their heat is more moderate than jalapeños. The green seed heads of garlic chives give this recipe special zip and flavor that are somewhat Asian in tone. Lacking garlic chives, substitute six sliced garlic cloves.

Yield: 2 quarts (2 liters)

1 pound (500g) freshly picked cauliflower

8 ounces (250g) freshly picked broccoli

1 large carrot (4 ounces/125g)

1 medium onion (about 8 ounces/125g), cut in half lengthwise, then thinly sliced

3 ounces (90g) fish peppers, mixed colors (15 to 20; or substitute another small hot pepper), seeded and sliced into thin strips or finely diced

9 seed heads of garlic chives, stems removed

2 tablespoons (20g) yellow mustard seeds, divided

1 cup (250ml) white wine vinegar

2 tablespoons (30g) kosher sea salt

¾ cup (185g) organic sugar

Sterilize a wide-mouthed 2-quart (2-liter) jar and lid (or smaller jars and lids) in a large pot of lightly boiling water.

Remove and discard the cauliflower stem and break or cut the florets into bite-size pieces. Remove the broccoli florets from the stem and cut into pieces the same size as the cauliflower. Combine the cauliflower and broccoli florets in a large work bowl. Pare the carrot and slice it into thin coins, then trim the coins into ornamental shapes—make about 30 pieces. Poach the carrot shapes in boiling water for 3 minutes, just until tender, then remove and run under cold water. Drain well, then add the carrots to the vegetable mixture along with the onion and peppers.

Place 3 garlic chive seed heads on the bottom of the prepared jar. Add ½ tablespoon (5g) of the mustard seeds, then pack half of the vegetable mixture into the jar, pressing gently with a wooden mallet. When half full, add another ½ tablespoon (5g) mustard seeds and 3 more seed heads. Fill with the remaining vegetable mixture and top with the remaining 1 tablespoon (10g) mustard seeds and seed heads (divide the ingredients evenly and repeat layering if using smaller jars).

Combine 3 cups (750ml) spring water with the vinegar, salt, and sugar in a medium nonreactive preserving pan. Bring to a full rolling boil over medium-high heat and boil for 3 minutes. Pour this over the vegetables and seal (see page 17).

Store in a cool dry place to allow the pickle to mature for about 3 weeks; refrigerate after opening. It will keep under refrigeration for up to 6 months, but it is preferable to use it sooner than that because due to the lack of chemical preservatives the cauliflower will begin to discolor and lose eye appeal.

Spicy Pumpkin Chutney

This chutney is intense, so I advise putting it up in smaller jars. It is meant to be very spicy, but for some the heat can overpower the other flavors. Add the hot pepper a few spoonfuls at a time until the heat level is where you want it. Of course, much will depend on the type of hot pepper—I used a cayenne during testing.

One more thing: Choose your pumpkin carefully. There are wonderful Chinese and Southeast Asian pumpkins with green flesh that are ideal for this chutney, yet sometimes difficult to find. A good fallback choice would be an acorn squash or a variety of pumpkin that bakes well. The point is to use one that will not dissolve quickly (like the orange field pumpkins sold for Halloween and Thanksgiving), but rather will hold together to give the chutney body and texture. I recommend the roasted walnut oil from La Tourangelle of Woodland, California.

Yield: 2 quarts (2 liters)

½ cup (125ml) roasted walnut oil, divided

1 teaspoon whole cumin seeds

2 teaspoons black mustard seeds

3½ cups (875g) organic sugar

2½ cups (625ml) white wine vinegar

2 tablespoons (50g) tamarind pulp (picked of seeds or seed fragments) or finely minced pitted dates

About 2 garlic cloves, cut lengthwise into 20 paper-thin slices

½ cup (100g) finely minced hot red pepper

1½ cups (190g) coarsely chopped walnuts

2 teaspoons ground cinnamon or 1 teaspoon ground cassia

2 teaspoons ground cardamom

2 tablespoons (50g) freshly grated ginger

1 tablespoon (15g) kosher sea salt

3½ pounds (about 1.5kg) firm, underripe winter squash or pumpkin (see headnote), peeled, seeded, flesh cut into small dice

Sterilize the jar(s), lid(s), and ring(s) in a large pot of lightly boiling water.

Heat ¼ cup (65ml) of the oil in a small heavy saucepan over medium heat. Once the oil is hot, add the cumin and mustard seeds and toast in the oil until they begin to crackle and pop. Remove the saucepan from the heat and set aside to cool.

Meanwhile, combine the sugar and vinegar in a large nonreactive preserving pan, stirring to dissolve the sugar. Whisk in the tamarind pulp and set over medium heat. Bring just to a boil and cook until the mixture becomes thick and syrupy, 10 to 15 minutes.

While the liquid is cooking, combine the garlic, hot pepper, walnuts, cinnamon, cardamom, ginger, and salt in a small bowl. Once the liquid is reduced to a thick syrup, add the pumpkin and stir to coat. Stir in the garlic mixture along with the cooled oil and toasted cumin and mustard seeds, increase the heat to medium-high, and cook steadily until the pumpkin is clear but not soft, 20 to 25 minutes. Stir up from the bottom of the pan from time to time to make sure the pumpkin cooks evenly and prevent scorching. Add the remaining ¼ cup (60ml) walnut oil, then transfer to the prepared jars and seal (see page 17). While it will keep for 2 or up to 3 years in a cool, dark place, the pickle is best when used within 9 months. Refrigerate after opening.

Spicy Green Tomato Chutney

This Indian-style pickle is excellent with rice and grilled meat or lamb. The recipe's elegance is that most of the ingredients are sliced paper-thin, which creates layers of texture and flavors—carefully use a very sharp knife or mandoline.

Yield: 2 quarts (2 liters)

1½ pounds (750g) firm green tomatoes, thinly sliced

½ medium onion (about 4 ounces/125g), cut in half lengthwise, then thinly sliced

½ lemon, thinly sliced and seeds removed

½ cup (100g) goji berries

4 large green jalapeño peppers (or green Punjabi peppers), seeded and thinly sliced

1 tablespoon (10g) diced fresh ginger

1 teaspoon whole cardamom seeds (removed from pods)

2 teaspoons ground star anise

1¼ cups (310g) organic sugar

3 cups (750ml) distilled white vinegar

1½ tablespoons (25g) kosher sea salt

Sterilize a wide-mouthed 2-quart (2-liter) canning jar, lid, and ring in a large pot of lightly boiling water. Or use several smaller jars, such as 4 pint (500ml) jars.

In a deep work bowl, combine the tomatoes, onion, lemon, goji berries, hot peppers, ginger, cardamom seeds, and star anise and stir to combine. Transfer to the prepared preserving jar or jars.

Combine the sugar, vinegar, 1 cup (250ml) spring water, and the salt in a large nonreactive preserving pan and bring to a rolling boil over medium-high heat. Boil for 3 minutes, then pour over the vegetable mixture and tightly close by hand—you don't need to microwave to seal

Store in the refrigerator or in a cool pantry out of direct sunlight to let mellow for at least 3 weeks before serving. The vegetables will shrink as they marinate, so be certain that they are sufficiently covered with brine. This pickle will keep under refrigeration for up to 2 years.

Kashmiri-Style Spicy Kale Chutney

This recipe is based on the traditional karam saag of Kashmir, a collard that I now grow at Roughwood (see Sources, page 199). I have taken my cue from the novel cuisine of Atul Kochhar whose chutneys at Benares in London first challenged my palate many years ago. While indeed a puree, it's also sour and spicy, and thus an excellent condiment for many types of foods—especially those with crispy textures like fried fish, toasted breads, or even chapatis.

This richly flavored cabbage is almost unknown outside of India and so delicate that it is treated in local cookery like spinach—hence the use of *saag*, which means "spinach." If you cannot locate the greens in a local market, or don't have them in your own kitchen garden, then follow the recipe below by using half kale and half baby spinach. Be sure to use a delicate kale, such as the young leaves of black Tuscan palm tree kale, sometimes known as dinosaur kale (a misnomer because, sadly, the dinosaurs never knew it).

Yield: About 1 quart (1 liter)

⅓ cup (90ml) virgin (cold-pressed) sesame oil

3 medium onions (about 1½ pounds/750g), cut in half lengthwise, then thinly sliced

4 large garlic cloves, minced

¾ cup (125g) finely chopped hot green peppers, the hotter the better

1 pound (500g) *karam saag* (or combine 8 ounces/250g delicate kale and 8 ounces/250g baby spinach; see headnote)

¾ cup (180ml) white wine vinegar

½ cup (125g) packed fresh cilantro, (leaves only)

1½ tablespoons (25g) kosher sea salt

1½ tablespoons (30g) freshly grated ginger

1 tablespoon (5g) ground coriander

2 teaspoons ground cumin

1 teaspoon ground mace

1 teaspoon ground anise

Sterilize the jar(s), lid(s), and ring(s) in a large pot of lightly boiling water.

In a wide sauté pan, heat the oil over medium-high heat just until it begins to crackle. Add the onions, then cover, reduce the heat to medium, and sweat the onions until soft, about 5 minutes.

Add the garlic, hot peppers, and *karam saag* (or kale and baby spinach). Stir in 1 cup (250ml) spring water and the vinegar. Cover and continue cooking over medium heat until the greens are soft, about 10 more minutes, then remove from the heat.

Transfer the hot greens and all the liquid to a food processor or high-speed blender and add the cilantro. Process until all the ingredients are reduced to a smooth puree, 1 to 2 minutes, then transfer to a clean work bowl.

Add the salt, ginger, coriander, cumin, mace, and anise and stir to combine. Transfer the mixture to a large nonreactive preserving pan and bring to a full boil over medium-high heat. Transfer the hot batter to the prepared jar(s) and tightly close by hand—you don't need to microwave to seal. Turn the closed jars upside-down and let stand for 5 minutes, then return upright and let cool. Within 5 to 10 minutes, you should hear the pop indicating the seal was successful. This will store well for 6 months in a cool, dark pantry.

Spicy Yellow Tomato Catsup

The best tomatoes for this type of recipe are paste tomatoes because of their lower water content. Years ago, because my grandmother had acid issues with the reds and frankly there wasn't a decent yellow paste tomato out there on the market, I bred a yellow paste tomato now called the Roughwood Golden Plum (see Sources, page 199). Hartman's Yellow Gooseberry is an heirloom variety with great flavor but cooking it down will take longer than my Golden Plum. Regardless, you can use any yellow tomato in this recipe; just be certain to start out with the amount of puree called for—you will need at least 8 quarts (dry measure) of tomatoes for the puree. I used an heirloom variety of hot pepper called Buist's yellow cayenne, but the *aji limó* or *aji amarillo* mentioned elsewhere will also work just as well. Their heat will mellow as the catsup ages, so batches made using those peppers are best consumed within six months. If you cannot find (or grow) fresh hot peppers, you can substitute 1 tablespoon (5 grams) ground *aji amarillo*, which is available in some specialty markets or online.

Yield: 2½ quarts (2.5 liters)—I usually use a few small catsup bottles

2½ quarts (2.5 liters) yellow tomato puree

(4½ pounds/2.25kg whole fresh yellow tomatoes cooked over medium-low heat until thickened, then passed through a sieve, strainer, or food mill to remove skins and seeds)

1 mango (about 1 pound/500g), peeled and chopped

¼ cup (60g) kosher sea salt

1¼ cups (315ml) white wine vinegar

½ cup (60g) seeded and diced hot yellow peppers

1½ cups (375g) organic sugar

1 tablespoon (25g) finely minced garlic

1 tablespoon (25g) freshly grated ginger

2 tablespoons (10g) fresh thyme leaves, or more to taste

Sterilize the jar(s) or bottle(s), lid(s), and ring(s) if using in a large pot of lightly boiling water.

Combine the tomato puree, mango, salt, vinegar, hot peppers, sugar, garlic, and ginger in a deep nonreactive preserving pan. Place over medium heat and cook until the mango is soft, about 15 minutes.

Remove from the heat, stir in the thyme leaves, and transfer the mixture in a blender, preferably a high-speed blender (thoroughly wash and dry the preserving pan). Blend the batter to a thick puree, 1 to 2 minutes.

Transfer the batter back to the clean preserving pan and return to medium heat. Continue to cook until the catsup achieves the consistency you desire, at least 20 minutes—some prefer their catsup thinner; others, thicker.

Transfer to the prepared jar(s) and seal (see page 17). The catsup will keep at least 1 year stored in a cool, dark place. Refrigerate after opening.

Zucchini Corn Relish

This versatile recipe is a variation of my grandmother's zucchini relish, which she continued to make until age ninety-six. The relish can be spiced any number of ways; in fact, chopped or sliced hot peppers can be added (to taste) instead of the powdered chiles for brighter heat. Sliced seeded pods of violet *buena mulata* (available from the Baker Creek Heirloom Seed Company, see Sources, page 199) are especially great here, both for their vivid color and excellent spicy flavor. For a different flavor profile, omit the turmeric and celery seeds in favor of 2 tablespoons (30g) whole cumin seeds and 2 tablespoons (10g) ground chipotle pepper.

Yield: 4 quarts (4 liters)

6 cups (750g) finely diced mature zucchini

3 cups (375g) corn kernels, cut from the cob (about 6 fresh ears)

4 cups (600g) finely diced onion

1½ cups (200g) finely diced green bell pepper

1½ cups (200g) finely diced red bell pepper

½ cup (125g) kosher sea salt

3 cups (750g) organic sugar

2½ cups (625ml) white wine vinegar

2 tablespoons (10g) ground turmeric

2 tablespoons (20g) whole celery seeds

1 tablespoon (5g) ground extra-hot pepper (Indian or Korean recommended), or to taste

Sterilize the jar(s), lid(s), and ring(s) in a large pot of lightly boiling water.

Combine the zucchini, corn, onion, and bell peppers in a deep work bowl and stir in the salt to coat the vegetables thoroughly. Cover the vegetable mixture with cold water and ice cubes. Let stand uncovered at room temperature for 1 hour, then drain well in a colander.

Transfer the vegetables to a large nonreactive preserving pan. In a saucepan, combine the sugar, vinegar, 1 cup (250ml) spring water, and the turmeric and bring to a full rolling boil over medium-high heat. Cook for 3 minutes, then pour the hot brine over the vegetables. Stir in the celery seeds and chile powder and simmer over medium heat until the zucchini is tender but not soft, about 15 minutes.

Transfer to the prepared jar(s) and seal (see page 17). This will keep for up to 3 years if stored in a cool, dark place, but is best used within 9 months. Refrigerate after opening.

02

Salty or Fermented

Without a doubt, salting and fermenting are among the oldest and most traditional methods of food preservation. There are a great many books devoted to this subject, and now that we also know that fermented foods are good for our digestive tracts, the dimension of health and wellness enters the discussion. Most Mediterranean-style pickles rely primarily on salt, and if vinegar is also used, normally there is no sugar.

If the first part of this book focuses on hot and spicy recipes from South America and India, this chapter shifts the focus to ingredients closer to European culinary traditions. *Alsatian Gumbisch* (page 70), Katia's Siberian Brined Tomatoes (page 89), and Cypriot Brine-Cured Green Olives (page 73)—these are all recipes that in some form or other require salt for success. Salt that is free of impurities and slow, controlled enzyme reactions are the secrets to the recipes in this chapter.

From the other side of globe come the subtleties of Asian-style pickles. I am quite partial to the Japanese tradition of pickled foods, often making a light meal of a salty or fermented pickle eaten with rice. And, since I grow my own bamboo, it became imperative that I learn how to pickle the shoots—there is nothing like the flavor of your own bamboo harvest, and a world of difference when you compare it to the texture and flavor of commercially canned bamboo shoots.

Alsatian *Gumbisch*

Gumbisch (or *Kumbisch*) was brought to the New World by Pennsylvania Dutch settlers from Alsace and neighboring areas of southwest Germany and Switzerland. As health food, *gumbisch* is particularly gut-friendly because its rich nutritional value is quickly absorbed into the body—which is is why it was sometimes called the peasant's apothecary. It corrected many dietary shortcomings; thus some peasant farmers viewed it as preventive medicine. As a result of their antimicrobial properties and natural catalysts, which give the dish its special flavor, juniper berries are critical to the success of this recipe.

Most traditional *gumbisch* recipes call for Savoy cabbage, mainly because it was that cabbage variety that grew best under the harsh conditions of the Alsatian hill country. However, Early Etampes and Cannonball cabbages are perfect for this recipe because of their small, compact shape (see the photo opposite). As Savoy cabbage (*chou frisé*) contains more fiber than common French cabbage (*chou blanc*), it needs poaching first, then salting, which makes the outcome somewhat different from typical sauerkraut (in fact, I prefer it to sauerkraut), and notably milder. Because it was considered a poverty dish, *gumbisch* rarely appeared in traditional cookbooks or on restaurant menus; however, its unique flavor recommends its revival and the culinary possibilities are many. Some old recipes call for dried sloes (wild plums), so once you perfect *gumbisch*, you can get creative—and if you are a kimchi fan, hot peppers and onions can be added. The leftover cabbage-poaching liquid can be used as the base for a hearty vegetable soup.

Yield: 6 pounds (3kg) or 3 gallons (12 liters)

6 pounds (3kg) Savoy cabbage (about 4 heads)

1 tablespoon (15g) plain sea salt

¼ cup (60g) kosher sea salt

¼ cup (20g) juniper berries

20 whole cloves

10 fresh bay leaves, bruised

Sterilize a wide-mouthed 3-gallon (12-liter) lidded crock in a large pot of lightly boiling water.

In a large stockpot, bring 6 quarts (5.75 liters) of water to a rolling boil over high heat and add the plain sea salt. Immediately reduce the heat so the water goes down to a very gentle simmer.

Cut each head of cabbage lengthwise into neat quarters or eighths, leaving the root ends intact so the pieces stay together. Add one head (in sections) to the simmering water and poach for 5 minutes, or until visibly wilted. Transfer to the prepared crock and repeat with remaining cabbage.

Add the kosher salt, juniper berries, cloves, and bay leaves and 1 gallon (4 liters) spring water to the cabbage and stir. Cover and allow the cabbage to ferment in a warm place for 2 weeks, then 3 weeks in a cold closet, or until the cabbage attains the desired texture and flavor. This pickle will keep over the winter in a cool, dark place but should be used by spring.

Brine-Cured Green Almonds (*Tsagala*)

I wish I could brag that I grow my own almonds, but the fickle Pennsylvania weather destroyed even my thirty-year-old fig tree (another victim of global warming), so I must rely on the annual appearance of green almonds flown in from Lebanon. The season is very short—two weeks in April—and then they are gone again. Many stores specializing in Middle Eastern foods carry the almonds in season because there is such high demand for them—they can be eaten raw as an appetizer, cooked, preserved in sugar, or pickled. I have cut back on the salt in this recipe and, on the advice of a Cypriot friend, added a little honey. The result is not as strong as your typical village pickle, and over time the almonds will change color and darken, so it is best consumed within one year. Follow the process on facing page if you prefer a more traditional brine.

Yield: 2 quarts (2 liters)

2 pounds (1kg) green almonds, washed

¼ cup (20g) whole coriander seeds

1 medium onion (about 8 ounces/250g), cut in half lengthwise, then thinly sliced

10 fresh bay leaves

1 teaspoon whole cloves

3 Ceylon cinnamon sticks

4 cups (1 liter) white wine vinegar

1 cup (250ml) honey

¼ cup (60g) organic sugar

1 tablespoon (15g) kosher sea salt

Sterilize a 2-quart (2-liter) jar, lid, and ring in a large pot of lightly boiling water.

Trim the stems from the almonds, then pierce them with a skewer on the stem end and insert the skewer almost to the other end. Do this to each almond and then combine the almonds, coriander seeds, onion, bay leaves, and cloves in a work bowl.

Put one of the cinnamon sticks in the bottom of the prepared jar and add half of the almond mixture. Add another cinnamon stick and fill with the remaining almond mixture. Top with the third cinnamon stick.

In a medium nonreactive preserving pan, combine the vinegar, honey, sugar, and salt. Place over medium-high heat and bring to a full rolling boil. Boil for 3 minutes, then pour the hot brine over the almonds and seal (see page 17).

Store in a cool place for at least 1 month before using. The cured almonds will keep for about 1 year.

Cypriot Brine-Cured Green Olives

While visiting the village of Skarinou on Cyprus more than ten years ago, I had the pleasure of spending the day harvesting olives with Andrea "Dagi" Kyprianou. He walked me through several traditional methods of brining, and this recipe is fairly close to one that he shared. Of course, he had vast amounts of many different varieties of fresh olives. I must settle for green olives flown in from California, but they're worth seeking out because homemade olives are much better than commercial olives, which are processed with lye and other chemical additives.

Yield: 6 pounds (3kg) olives

6 pounds (3kg) green olives

1 cup (80g) whole coriander seeds

10 whole cloves

3 tablespoons (15g) crumbled dried *rigani* (Cypriot oregano) or Greek oregano

10 fresh bay leaves

1 cup (225g) kosher sea salt

2 cups (500ml) white wine vinegar

Wash the olives, picking out any that are bruised or damaged—adding more olives to be certain you maintain 6 pounds (3 kg). Put them in a deep 2- to 3-gallon (8- to 12-liter) lidded crock. Add the coriander seeds, cloves, *rigani*, and bay leaves and stir well to combine.

In a large nonreactive preserving pan, bring 1-gallon (4 liters) spring water to a gentle boil, then add the salt and immediately turn off the heat. Let the water cool to room temperature and let the salt fully dissolve. Stir in the vinegar, then pour the brine over the olives. Place a dish on the surface of the olives in the crock to weigh them down just below the level of the brine and cover the crock with the lid.

Set away to ferment for 2 months, checking occasionally for mold or escaped olives. Once fermentation ceases, allow the flavor to develop over the course of 2 to 4 more months, depending on the precise taste you want. After 2 months, the flavor will be mild. If allowed to stand longer, the olives will undergo more change, gradually growing saltier and more intensely flavored; their color will also darken. The olives will keep without refrigeration for at least 1 year if stored well covered in a cool place.

Ceviche Sauce (*Salsa par Escabeche*)

This pungent sauce is based on fermented *aji escabeche*, the classic Andean pepper that has made Peruvian ceviche so famous. An ancient pepper dating back to precolonial times, *aji escabeche* is a member of the *baccatum* species and thus features fruity flavors not found in other peppers. One eats these raw with *vinho verde* to savor their unique complexity; thus it follows that a light white wine should serve as the base for this fermented sauce.

My strain of *aji escabeche* is extremely mild; most ripe pods have no heat at all. In fact, the pepper's young green pods are quite hot; but, as they ripen to red, they lose their heat. When ripe, the pepper's flavor shows hints of banana and cherry, and salsas made with it can go in several flavor directions. Here, I have opted to blend it with a small Andean red pepper belonging to the *chinense* species, called *aji charapita rojo*, which contributes both subtle smokiness and gentle heat. Ultimately, this sauce is intended to marry well with grilled fish and meats, so keep it simple: Think of this as a base on which to build many different marinade variations. Seeds for both peppers are available from the Roughwood Seed Collection (see Sources, page 199).

Yield: About 2 quarts (2 liters)—I usually use several small catsup bottles

1 pound (500g) trimmed and seeded ripe *aji escabesche* (weight after trimming and seeding)

4 ounces (125g) trimmed and seeded ripe *aji charapita rojo* or any red *chinense* pepper (weight after trimming and seeding)

¼ cup (60g) kosher sea salt

2 cups (500ml) dry white wine, such as *vinho verde*

1½ cups (375ml) red wine vinegar

1½ cups (375ml) Coriander Vinegar (page 199)

1 tablespoon (5g) ground cumin

Grated zest of 1 lime

Sterilize the jar(s), lid(s), and ring(s), or bottle(s) in a large pot of lightly boiling water.

Combine both peppers in a food processor or high-speed blender with 2 cups (500ml) spring water and process into a thick puree, 1 to 2 minutes. Add the salt. This should yield about 1 quart (1 liter) puree.

Transfer the puree into the prepared jar(s) or bottle(s). Add the wine and mix thoroughly. Cover with cheesecloth and set aside in a cool place to ferment for 3 weeks. Check on the fermentation, stirring every other day to prevent mold from forming. While the mash ferments, prepare the coriander vinegar.

At the end of the 3 weeks, when the mash ceases to bubble, pass both mash and brine through a fine strainer and discard the solids.

To each 2 cups (500ml) of brine, add ½ cup (125ml) red wine vinegar and ½ cup (125ml) coriander vinegar. Stir in the cumin and lime zest, then transfer to freshly cleaned and prepared jar(s) or bottle(s), close lids tightly, and refrigerate. If you prefer to seal the containers for longer storage, allow 15 minutes for a water bath. Either way the salsa will keep for at least 3 years and actually improves from aging.

Brine-Cured Turnips and Horseradish

This is a fermented pickle that follows the same basic method as sauerkraut. It is easy to make and freezes especially well. As in many other recipes in this section, the process is called lacto-fermentation because the enzyme change follows the same path as that in cheese—the white mold you may see on some cheeses is the same one in operation here.

Yield: 5 to 6 pounds (2.5 to 3kg)

1 pound (500g) shredded white cabbage

3 tablespoons (45g) kosher sea salt

1½ tablespoons (15g) yellow mustard seeds

1 pound (500g) onions, cut in half lengthwise, then thinly sliced

1 pound (500g) daikon radish, pared and shredded on the large holes of a grater

2½ pounds (1.25kg) white turnips, pared and shredded on the large holes of a grater

½ cup (50g) finely shredded fresh horseradish

2 tablespoons (50g) freshly grated ginger

2 tablespoons (50g) Dijon mustard

1 tablespoon (10g) caraway seeds

Sour cream, for serving

Chopped chives or green onions, for serving

Using your hands, combine the shredded cabbage with the salt and mustard seeds, squeezing vigorously so the cabbage is bruised and slightly limp (see Flaming Kimchi, page 84). Mix in the onions, radish, and turnip, continuing to squeeze until tender, then stir in the horseradish.

Transfer to a 3-gallon (12-liter) stoneware crock and pound with a wooden kraut stomper to pack the ingredients as tightly as possible. Place a china dish upside-down on top of the mixture. Press down and set a weight on top of the plate (a large jar of water will work—whatever you choose should weigh at least 4 pounds/2kg). Pour in enough spring water to cover the dish.

Place a cloth over the crock and stand it in a warm spot for about 1 week (depending on the weather—hot weather will cause it to ferment more quickly), until the mixture begins to undergo an enzyme change—your nose will tell you. Move the crock to a cool place for at least 10 days to encourage the lacto-fermentation to continue slowly. If left in a warm place, the ferment will spoil, so it is necessary to slow it down.

After 10 days, skim off any mold that has formed on the top and test the ferment. If the vegetables seem a little raw, continue fermentation until you are happier with the texture. When the vegetables are tender, add the ginger, mustard, and caraway seeds.

Pack the mixture with some of the liquid into resealable freezer bags, then date and label the bags and freeze until needed, reserving the portion of the mixture you want to enjoy immediately in a jar in the refrigerator. This pickle does not require cooking and is best served at room temperature as a side dish, mixed with sour cream and garnished with chopped chives or green onions.

Fermented Hot Pepper Sauce

Fermenting hot sauce is like winemaking, in that the same pepper can produce different results in different hands. The most important rule to follow: Use only ripe red peppers. If you're making sauce to go with fish and shellfish, try fish peppers or ripe *ajis escabeche* (see Ceviche Sauce, page 74), both known for pairing well with seafood. Fleshy elephant trunk peppers make excellent sauce for grilled meats; and, if you like smokiness, any *Capsicum chinense* will suit, including the habanero, Scotch bonnet, Cumari, or Peruvian *miscuchu*. Based on what you intend your sauce to go with, you can tweak the seasonings further—a little grated orange zest if it's duck; minced rosemary for a spicy grilled goat sauce, and so forth. Whichever pepper and optional flavorings you choose, be certain the vinegar is well flavored with garlic to add complexity to the heat. For this recipe, I use an organic cider made in the Basque region of Spain called Gurutzeta; it comes with its own lees, which help promote healthy fermentation.

Yield: About 2 quarts (2 liters)—I usually use four 16-ounce (500-ml) catsup bottles

2 pounds (1kg) trimmed and seeded hot red peppers (weight after trimming and seeding)

6 tablespoons (90g) kosher sea salt

3 cups (750ml) dry hard cider (see headnote)

About 3 cups (750ml) Garlic Vinegar (page 194)

Sterilize a 2-quart (2-liter) wide-mouthed canning jar in a saucepan of lightly boiling water.

Puree the peppers in a food processor or blender—you should have about 1 quart (1 liter) of puree, then add the salt. Transfer the puree to the prepared canning jar and add the hard cider. Cover the jar with cheesecloth and set aside in a cool place to ferment. The same day you start the peppers, make the garlic vinegar.

Ferment the pepper mixture for 3 weeks (21 days), stirring every other day to prevent mold from forming. Beyond 3 weeks, fermentation time becomes a matter of personal taste, so ask yourself of just how much change you want the flavors to undergo—the older it ages, the smoother it becomes. Once fermented as desired, press the mash and brine through a food mill or strainer, discarding the solids—you should have about 6 cups (1.5 liters) of pepper brine. To each 1 cup (250ml) pepper brine, add ½ cup (125ml) garlic vinegar.

Sterilize four 16-ounce (500-ml) catsup bottle(s) or jar(s), lid(s), and ring(s) in a large saucepan of lightly boiling water.

Adjust the seasonings, then transfer the mixture to bottles, close the lids tightly, and refrigerate.

If you prefer to can the sauce, allow a 15-minute water bath for small bottles (do not use the microwave method for this one).

Crock Pickles with Dill and Garlic

This is a delicious and uncomplicated traditional pickle prepared according to the raw-pack method. Before the advent of home canning, pickles were simply placed in a stoneware crock in a cool pantry, covered, mellowed in brine, and then kept until needed during the course of the winter. This recipe can also be used with green tomatoes, mixed green and sweet red peppers, poached carrots, poached radishes, and several other sorts of vegetables, even cabbage. The red pepper is essentially ornamental, but some people like to add hot pepper instead. It is essential to let the pickle stand for three weeks before using to allow the vegetables to undergo lacto-fermentation, which is important both for flavor and texture.

Yield: 2 quarts (2 liters)

1 tablespoon (10g) yellow mustard seeds

8 fresh bay leaves

2 tablespoons (10g) whole coriander seeds

1 large bunch fresh dill (15g), preferably with at least some flower heads

2 pounds (1kg) small pickling cucumbers (about 12 to 16, each 4 inches/10cm long), trimmed and halved lengthwise

10 garlic cloves, cut in half lengthwise

½ red bell pepper, cut into thin strips, optional

1 cup (250ml) white wine vinegar, or, preferably, Garlic or Shallot Vinegar (page 194)

¼ cup (60g) kosher sea salt

Sterilize a wide-mouthed 2-quart (2-liter) canning jar, lid, and ring in a large pot of lightly boiling water.

Combine the mustard seeds, bay leaves, and coriander seeds in a small bowl. Place half of the dill in the bottom of the prepared jar. Pack the cucumbers into the jar, standing them on end with cut sides facing out. Pack the spice mixture, garlic, and red pepper around the cucumbers, ending with the remaining dill on top.

Combine 1 quart (1 liter) spring water, the vinegar, and salt in a large nonreactive preserving pan. Place over medium-high heat, bring to a rolling boil, and boil for 3 minutes. Pour the hot brine over the cucumbers and cover loosely with a lid—do not seal; lacto-fermentation may cause the jar to explode. Transfer the jar to the refrigerator and let the pickles mature for 3 weeks before using—this wait allows the flavors of all the ingredients to blend and heighten. (You may tighten the lid at this point.) The pickles will keep under refrigeration for up to 2 years, but are best consumed within 9 months.

Brine-Cured Cornelian Cherries

The cherries are brined following a recipe for olives from Cyprus. Choose a variety with olive-shaped fruit and harvest them right before they begin to change color. For larger batches, the recipe can be doubled or quadrupled. Cornelian cherries are not true cherries, rather the cherry-like fruit from a tree related to dogwood—sacred to Apollo, this tree played a decisive role in the Trojan Wars. Out of hand, the red or yellow cherries are extremely sour and not to be eaten fresh. The green fruit resemble olives in shape, down even to an olive-like pit, thus they can be treated as olives in regions where true olives cannot be grown.

Yield: 3 pounds (1.5 kg)

3 pounds (1.5kg) green Cornelian cherries, stemmed and rinsed

½ cup (40g) whole coriander seeds

5 whole cloves

5 fresh bay leaves

1½ tablespoons (7g) crumbled dried *rigani* (Cypriot oregano) or Greek oregano

½ cup (125g) kosher sea salt

1 cup (250ml) white wine vinegar

3 tablespoons (45g) pickling salt, optional

5 garlic cloves, sliced, optional

1½ teaspoons whole cloves, optional

Wash the cherries, picking out any that may be bruised or damaged. Add more cherries to be certain you have 3 pounds (1.5 kg). Combine the cherries, coriander seeds, cloves, bay leaves, and *rigani* in a clean 1-gallon (4-liter) glass jar.

In a large nonreactive preserving pan, bring 2 quarts (2 liters) spring water to a gentle boil over medium heat and add the kosher salt. Remove from the heat and let cool just until the pot is cool enough to handle but the water is still hot. Add the vinegar and pour the hot brine over the cherries. (Note that, unlike olives, the cherries won't float, making it unnecessary to weigh them down with a plate.)

Cover loosely with a lid and set away in a cool, dark place for 2 months to undergo slow fermentation. Check once a week on the status of mold and skim it off if any should develop. After 2 months, once fermentation stops, allow the flavors to develop further over 2 to 4 months, depending on the precise flavor you want to achieve. For best flavor, after 2 months, add the pickling salt and garlic. After another month, add the cloves. The cherries will keep for at least 1 year if kept well covered in a cool place away from direct sunlight.

Cauliflower and Broccoli Pickle with Olives and Fennel

If you do not have fresh fennel in the garden, use fennel seeds and fennel greens stripped from Florence fennel (bulb fennel). Young fennel blossoms are always best, especially when the flowers are just beginning to set young green seeds, which is when freshly harvested fennel is most flavorful. Lacking fennel, you can make this recipe with dill.

Yield: 2 quarts (2 liters)

8 ounces (250g) freshly picked cauliflower, broken into small bite-size florets (weight after coring)

8 ounces (250g) freshly picked broccoli florets

4 ounces (125g) pearl onions, peeled and halved lengthwise

2 large garlic cloves, each sliced lengthwise into 4 to 5 pieces

40 large unpitted brine-cured green olives (Castelvetranos or a similar variety)

4 fresh bay leaves

6 whole cloves

2 tablespoons (20g) yellow mustard seeds

3 tablespoons (30g) whole fennel seeds (or dill seeds)

20 small rings sweet pepper (preferably orange)

2 small bunches fresh fennel or dill greens with flower heads and green seeds

3 cups (750ml) white wine vinegar

⅔ cup (155g) organic sugar

¼ cup (60g) kosher sea salt

Sterilize the jar(s), lid(s), and ring(s) in a large pot of lightly boiling water.

Combine the cauliflower, broccoli, pearl onions, garlic, olives, bay leaves, cloves, mustard seeds, fennel seeds, and sweet pepper rings in a large work bowl. Place 1 bunch of the fennel or dill greens in the bottom of the prepared jar. Add the vegetable mixture and top with the remaining greens.

In a nonreactive medium preserving pan, combine the vinegar, 1½ cups (375ml) spring water, the sugar, and salt. Place over medium heat and bring to a rolling boil for about 3 minutes, then pour the hot brine over the vegetables and seal (see page 17).

Let the pickle mature for 30 days before serving. This will keep in a cool, dark place for up to 1 year; however, since the recipe is all-natural with no preservatives, the cauliflower will begin to darken after 6 to 9 months, so you may prefer to use it before then.

Flaming Kimchi

This will only be as "flaming" as you want it. Personally, I like it super-hot, practically boiling with peppers around the edges, if boiling could actually be tasted. Most recipes for kimchi made with Napa cabbage are fairly straightforward, as the structure is consistent within certain basic proportions, such as that of salt to cabbage, for example. Where the fun begins is in the elaboration, the addition of flavorful ingredients—in this case, the peppers designed to make this kimchi spicy-hot the way many Koreans like it. If you prefer to douse the flames, so to speak, then simply leave out the *gochugaru* listed below. The *gochugaru* gives the kimchi both color and flavor; the pureed hot peppers provide the heat.

Adding green onions during fermentation (as called for in many recipes) often results in an unpleasant grassy taste and slimy texture, not to mention that they can go off very easily. I suggest only adding them the night before you plan to serve the kimchi or even just a few hours beforehand. That way, they will retain their freshness and distinct texture. Finally, make sure to use spring water in the first step—tap water contains many impurities, even traces of antibiotics, which could affect the outcome of the fermentation process.

Yield: 1 quart (1 liter)

½ cup (125g) kosher sea salt

2½ pounds (1.25kg) Napa cabbage, chopped into bite-size pieces

8 ounces (250g) turnip or daikon radish, shredded or cut into fine matchsticks

1 tablespoon (25g) finely minced garlic

1 tablespoon (20g) freshly grated ginger

¼ cup (60ml) Korean salted shrimp (*saeujeot*) or fish sauce.

⅓ cup (30g) Korean chile flakes (*gochugaru*)

1 tablespoon (15g) pureed hot red peppers

2 teaspoons organic sugar

3 green onions, cut into 1-inch lengths, optional

Toasted sesame oil for drizzling, optional

1 tablespoon (9g) toasted sesame seeds, or to taste, optional

Sterilize a 1-quart (1-liter) jar in a pot of lightly boiling water.

Dissolve the salt in 2 quarts (2 liters) spring water. Place the chopped cabbage in a deep nonreactive container and add the brine. Cover with a clean plate and top with a weight (such as a clean 1-quart/1-liter jar full of water) to press the cabbage below the level of the water. Marinate the cabbage for at least 8 hours or overnight at room temperature. After it has marinated, drain the cabbage and squeeze out as much water as possible—this bruising action is important to the fermentation process and to the ultimate texture of the kimchi. Set the drained cabbage aside.

Combine the turnip, garlic, ginger, and salted shrimp in a large bowl. Add the Korean chile flakes, pureed hot peppers, and sugar and toss gently until a paste forms. Using your hands, work with a squeezing action to combine the reserved cabbage with the turnip paste. Put the mixture into the prepared jar and press with a weight. Let the kimchi ferment for 1 week in a cool place. The cabbage should be very soft, as though partially cooked.

The kimchi recipe will keep in the refrigerator for up to 1 month. For best flavor and texture, serve the kimchi shortly after it's made and make fresh batches as needed. If desired, add green onions, toasted sesame oil, or toasted sesame seeds before serving.

Japanese-Style Pickled Eggplant with *Shiso* (*Shibazuki*)

For best results, use long, narrow Japanese or Asian eggplants, preferably varieties with white or pink skin, 13 to 14 inches (32.5 to 35cm) long. Japanese-style cucumbers are firm and contain few seeds at early-harvest stage, and their texture is an important counterpoint to the eggplant. The red *shiso* (perilla) will color the pickle but must be harvested before it blooms, when the leaves are dark black-red, with no green on the undersides. *Shiso* takes several weeks to dye a pickle, so the longer the mixture can stand in the crock, the better. To strengthen the color and *shiso* flavor, I recommend adding more leaves later in the pickling process. This homemade version of *shibazuke* (salt-cured eggplant) avoids the artificial food coloring and a host of preservatives commonly found in commercially packaged versions.

Yield: 2 quarts (1 liter)

2 pounds (1 kg) Japanese or Asian eggplant

5 tablespoons (75g) kosher sea salt, divided

1 pound (500g) Japanese cucumbers, sliced into narrow (2-inch/5-cm) strips

2 cups (500ml) light soy sauce (*usukuchi shoyu*)

¼ cup (60g) organic sugar

About 6 cups (about 450g) red shiso (perilla) leaves, divided

½ cup (125ml) Red Shiso Vinegar (see page 197)

½ cup (125ml) mirin

1 cup (175g) prepared sushi ginger (drained of liquid)

Slice the eggplant on a diagonal as thinly as possible. Toss with 3 tablespoons (45g) salt and lay the slices in a colander set in a large bowl. Cover and let drain at room temperature. After 2 hours, discard the liquid; do not rinse the eggplant.

In a large, preserving crock or glass jar, combine the drained eggplant with the sliced cucumber, light soy sauce, remaining 2 tablespoons salt (30 g), sugar, and 4 cups (300g) of red perilla. Weigh down the eggplant mixture with a 4-pound (2kg) cover (the vegetables must be completely submerged), and marinate 10 days in a cool, dark cupboard or until the ingredients are tender and agreeable to taste.

Don't be concerned if the pickle begins to show white mold resembling oyster mushrooms—this is a sign of lacto-fermentation and also a sign that the pickle has fermented long enough and you should move to the next step.

Sterilize a 2-quart (2-liter) wide-mouthed canning jar, lid, and ring in a saucepan of lightly boiling water. Remove any mold floating on the surface of the pickling liquid, then drain the eggplant in a colander and save the brine. Transfer the drained pickle into a clean work bowl. Mix in the red shiso vinegar, mirin, and pickled ginger. As you pack the mixture into the prepared jar, pick out the spent shiso leaves (they will resemble cooked spinach) and mix in fresh leaves—or about half the amount from the original ferment. Pour the reserved brine over the pickle, cover with a canning lid, and twist the ring on tightly. Keep in the refrigerator or in a cool, dark place for up to 6 months.

Katia's Siberian Brined Tomatoes

This is an old family recipe of a friend of mine who hails from Tomsk, Siberia. The tomatoes are eaten more or less like a winter salad. The trick is to have the right balance of salt: just enough to preserve the tomatoes yet not make the final pickle overly briny. As with many traditional Russian recipes, the flavor of dill predominates. Small to medium tomatoes about 1½ inches (4cm) in diameter are best here. A mix of colors is especially attractive, and even green (unripe) tomatoes can be added.

Yield: 2 quarts (2 liters)

2 pounds (1kg) small tomatoes (about 30), enough to fill a half-gallon (2-liter) glass jar

2 large bunches fresh dill

6 fresh bay leaves

1 small bunch fresh parsley

4 garlic cloves, peeled and halved lengthwise

1 tablespoon (10g) whole black peppercorns

2 to 3 long hot peppers (left whole)

1 tablespoon (5g) whole coriander seeds

1 tablespoon (10g) whole dill seeds

5 tablespoons (75g) kosher sea salt

Sterilize the jar(s), lid(s), and ring(s) in a saucepan of lightly boiling water.

Wash and stem the tomatoes. With a skewer, pierce each tomato all the way through from the stem end to the blossom end—this creates a way for the brine to enter. Combine half of the dill with the bay leaves, parsley, garlic, peppercorns, hot peppers, coriander seeds, and dill seeds in the prepared jar. Add the tomatoes and place the remaining fresh dill on top.

In a large nonreactive preserving pan, bring 6 cups (1.5 liters) spring water to a rolling boil over medium-high heat. Add the salt and stir to dissolve.

Pour the hot brine over the tomato mixture and close the lids tightly. Store in a cool, dark place for at least 1 week before opening. Do not keep for more than 6 months.

Lemon-Brined Carrots

This pickle is especially attractive when made with different colored carrots, but keep in mind that if you use purple or red carrots, their color will gradually bleed into the brine and turn the pickle pink. If you prefer to accentuate that color, try rosé wine vinegar instead of white; but whatever color the pickle ends up, even the onions will be delicious! To enhance the lemony flavor, sprinkle with a little freshly grated lemon zest before serving. As an alternative, use oranges instead of lemons.

Yield: 1 quart (1 liter)

1 pound (500g) trimmed and pared carrots (weight after trimming and paring), cut into thin (1½-inch/(3.75-cm) sticks

2 medium onions (8 ounces/250g), cut in half lengthwise, then thinly sliced

1 teaspoon whole allspice

1 teaspoon whole black peppercorns

6 fresh bay leaves

Zest of 1 lemon, shaved with a vegetable peeler into 6 strips

⅓ cup (90ml) white wine vinegar

2 tablespoons (30g) kosher sea salt

Sterilize a wide-mouthed 1-quart (1-liter) canning jar, lid, and ring in a saucepan of lightly boiling water.

Bring another pot of water to a rolling boil over high heat, then add the carrots, reduce the heat to medium, and poach the carrots for 3 minutes, or until crisp-tender but not cooked through. Drain immediately and rinse under cold water, then drain well and set aside.

Combine the onions, allspice, and peppercorns in a deep work bowl. Place 2 bay leaves and 2 strips of lemon zest at the bottom of the prepared jar. Add half of the onion mixture and pack it down tightly with a wooden mallet or potato masher. Add 6 bay leaves and 6 lemon zest strips, then pack the poached carrots into the jar as tightly as possible, standing them on end. Top the carrots with the remaining bay leaves and strip of lemon zest, then cover with the remaining onion mixture. Add the last bay leaf and lemon zest on top and pack the mixture down again with wooden mallet or potato masher.

Stand the jar in a bowl of boiling water. In a large nonreactive preserving pan, combine 2 cups (500ml) spring water, the vinegar, and salt. Bring to a rolling boil and boil for 3 minutes. Pour the brine over the carrot mixture and close the lid tightly (no need to microwave).

Let the pickle mature for 2 to 3 weeks in a cool, dark place before using. Keep in a cool, dark place for up to 2 years, but this recipe is best consumed within 9 months.

Peruvian *Miscuchu* Marinade (*Adobo de Aji Miscuchu*)

Aji miscuchu is a photogenic golden yellow pepper with an ancient indigenous name. It hails from the jungles of eastern Peru, which may account for its up-front spiciness. On the other hand, the *miscuchu* pepper also features a subtle, fruity, banana-like flavor when eaten raw and the same distinctive smokiness as other *Capsicum chinense* species. As such, this Andean classic is to Peruvian cuisine what the habanero is to Caribbean cookery and is excellent as a sauce for any dish with plantains or sweet potatoes or added to soups and stews. As a fermented marinade, it is perfect for grilling fish, poultry, and potatoes. Furthermore, it makes an extraordinary marinade for roast turkey or duck.

Since the *miscuchu* pepper is quite hot, I have reigned in the proportion in relation to the sweet peppers in this recipe. I would describe the result as only mildly hot, although the gentle heat lingers. A chef friend observed that it "purrs," which is a good description. If you prefer a spicier sauce, I suggest adding pureed *miscuchu* peppers to the ferment in 2-ounce (60-g) intervals until the desired heat is achieved (taste as you add the peppers). When serving as a salsa, minced fresh *huacatay* always adds extra flavor—try mixing it with minced parsley and let guests season to taste. A little minced cilantro is nice as well.

Yield: About 7½ cups (about 2 liters)

2 pounds (1kg) trimmed and seeded sweet orange peppers (weight after trimming and seeding)

8 ounces (250g) trimmed and seeded *miscuchu* peppers (weight after trimming and seeding)

6 tablespoons (90g) kosher sea salt

Huacatay Vinegar (page 194)

1 tablespoon (5g) ground cumin

2 teaspoons powdered mustard

1 teaspoon ground mace

Sterilize a 2-quart (2-liter) canning jar and ring in a saucepan of lightly boiling water.

Puree both the sweet and hot peppers in a food processor or high-speed blender until reduced to a coarse cornmeal consistency. Transfer the puree to the prepared jar. Dissolve the salt in 2 cups (500ml) spring water and stir into the pepper puree. Cover the mouth of the jar with cheesecloth and stretch it tight, then cover with the ring. Set aside in a cool, dark place to ferment for 15 days (20 won't improve the flavor, so best to date the jar for accuracy), stirring it every other day to prevent mold. Should it develop a white tinge on top, immediately stir this into the fermenting batter. You will know it is fermenting because it will bubble and separate—keep mixing so it ferments evenly. Prepare the huacatay vinegar and let it marinate alongside the salsa.

At the end of 15 days, pass the fermented sauce through a food mill or strainer and discard the mash. Measure the liquid: To each 1 cup (250ml), add ½ cup (125ml) huacatay vinegar until you have 7½ cups (almost 2 liters). Mix in the ground cumin, mustard, and mace, then pour into the sterilized jar, cover tightly, and refrigerate.

As with most homemade salsas, this will separate once it stands for any length of time, so shake well before using.

Pickled Bamboo Shoots

Since this classic Chinese-inspired recipe is based on salt, I have included it in this section of the book even though it is not technically salt-cured. That said, this is a simple, straightforward pickle that preserves much of the flavor of the fresh shoots, which most commercial versions can't claim. Furthermore, this recipe represents the opposite of the Korean-Style Sweet and Sour Bamboo Shoots (page 140), because here the shoots are preserved in a mild, delicate brine, so the pickle can be used in combination with other ingredients, for example in stir-fries. Garlic enhances the natural flavor of bamboo, so there is a lot of it in this recipe, but one of the best optional ingredients is lemongrass or a few strips of lemon zest. I have added Szechuan peppercorns, but hot chiles or other spices can be added according to your preference. Thinly sliced fresh ginger is always a welcome addition, but don't overcomplicate the recipe because this pickle is most versatile when kept simple. Best of all, the flavor seems to improve with age, so let this stand for three months before opening.

Yield: 2 quarts (2 liters)—I usually use 2 narrow-mouthed 1-quart (1-liter) canning jars so the bamboo does not rise into the airspace at the top of the jar

2½ pounds (1.25kg) prepared (poached and trimmed) bamboo shoots, (weight after trimming)

8 large garlic cloves, each cut lengthwise into 3 slices (24 slices total)

2 tablespoons (10g) whole Szechuan peppercorns, or to taste

4 stalks fresh lemongrass, trimmed, or long strips of lemon zest to taste, optional

⅔ cup (160ml) unseasoned rice vinegar

½ cup (125ml) Shaoxing rice wine (or dry sherry)

¼ cup (60g) kosher sea salt

Sterilize the jar(s), lid(s), and ring(s) in a saucepan of lightly boiling water.

To yield trimmed, poached shoots ready for pickling: Fill a large nonreactive work bowl with cold water, add enough salt so the water is as salty as seawater, and set aside. Trim off about 1 inch (2cm) from the base of each bamboo shoot, then cut the shoots in half lengthwise. Strip off the outer leaves and immerse the tender hearts in the cold salt water. Exposure to air will toughen the shoots, so keep them submerged until ready to poach.

Transfer the trimmed shoots to a large nonreactive preserving pan and cover with fresh water. Bring to a gentle boil over medium heat and cook for 10 to 15 minutes (larger varieties will need longer). Remove and rinse under cold running water. Taste a small piece from one of the shoots, and if you can detect bitterness, repeat the previous step, but shorten cooking time to 5 to 8 minutes, depending on size. Once the bitterness has been neutralized, return the poached shoots to fresh salted water until you are ready to pickle.

Pack the prepared bamboo shoots, garlic, Szechuan peppercorns, and lemongrass or lemon zest, if using, into the prepared jar(s). In a large nonreactive preserving pan, combine 1 quart (1 liter) spring water, the vinegar, rice wine, and salt and bring to a rolling boil over medium-high heat. Pour the hot brine over the bamboo mixture and cover tightly. Let cool, transfer to the refrigerator, and store for at least 2 weeks before using.

The pickled shoots will keep under refrigeration for about 1 year before opening. They will also keep well in a cool, dark pantry.

Mediterranean-Style Pickled Cardoons

I have two varieties of cardoons in my garden at Roughwood. The *cardon genevois* from Switzerland thrives the best and supplies me with the ingredients for this recipe. Cardoons can be an acquired taste for those who have not grown up where sour, salty, and even bitter are common themes in pickle recipes. Basic Mediterranean-style pickles, whether Greek, Syrian, or otherwise, generally consist of one part vinegar and one part strong brine, with no sugar at all. This recipe follows that classic format and will taste very much like the style of pickled cardoons served on the Greek islands and elsewhere. The stems must be parboiled and then infused for two days to remove most of the bitterness. Eaten with other appetizers as part of a meze, pickled cardoons are often served with olive oil, a squeeze of lemon juice, and perhaps some chopped fennel. The pickled stems are also delicious cooked with green fava beans and snails. For best results, harvest only the youngest and most tender stems; mature stems are stringy and tough.

Yield: 1 quart (1 liter)

1 pound (500g) fresh cardoon stems, trimmed of leaves and tips

2 lemons plus 1 wide strip lemon zest

3½ tablespoons (55g) kosher sea salt, divided

1 teaspoon dried oregano

1 teaspoon whole coriander seeds

1 large garlic clove, halved lengthwise

2 cups (500ml) white wine vinegar

Place the trimmed cardoon stems in a deep nonreactive work bowl, preferably glass or stoneware. Juice the lemons to yield ½ cup (65ml) lemon juice; quarter and reserve the squeezed rinds. Dissolve 2 tablespoons (30g) of the salt in 6 cups (1.5 liters) spring water, add the lemon juice, then pour the brine over the cardoon stems. Add the lemon rinds, then cover and let stand in a cool place for 2 days.

After 2 days, sterilize the jar(s), lid(s), and ring(s) in a saucepan of lightly boiling water. Discard the brine and lemon rinds and cut the cardoon stems into 3-inch (7.5-cm) lengths, trimming off any parts that may have discolored.

Create an ice-water bath in a deep work bowl. In a large nonreactive preserving pan, bring 2 quarts (2 liters) water to a rolling boil over medium-high heat. Add the trimmed cardoon stems and cook for exactly 1 minute, then remove and immediately plunge into the ice-water bath. Drain well, then pack the blanched cardoon stems into the prepared jar(s) and add the oregano, coriander seeds, garlic, and lemon zest.

In a small nonreactive preserving pan, combine 1 cup (250ml) spring water, the vinegar, and the remaining 1½ tablespoons (25g) salt and bring to a boil over medium-high heat. Pour the brine over the cardoon stems and seal (see page 17). This pickle will keep for several years in a cool, dark closet but is best consumed before the end of 12 months.

Sauerkraut with Celeriac, Onion, and Carrot

This old-time Pennsylvania farmhouse classic deserves to be better known because it is delicious and totally different from common sauerkraut—and not as stinky either! The delicate balance of flavors makes this an excellent side dish with stewed meat, and when cooked with hard cider and raisins, it can dress up any holiday table. For best results, use a sanitized 3-gallon (12-liter) stoneware crock.

Yield: About 10 pounds (5 kilos)

7½ pounds (3.75kg) finely shredded white cabbage

1½ pounds (750g) finely shredded celeriac

1½ pounds (750g) thinly sliced onion

12 ounces (375g) finely shredded carrot

4½ tablespoons (68g) kosher sea salt

Divide each of the ingredient totals into three equal portions: You will fill the crock with three even layers of the combined ingredients. Once divided, combine 2½ pounds (1.25kg) cabbage, 8 ounces (250g) celeriac, 8 ounces (250g) sliced onion, 4 ounces (125g) carrot, and 1½ tablespoons (25g) salt in a deep work bowl. Using your hands, squeeze the mixture vigorously so the ingredients are slightly bruised; this bruising action is important to the fermentation process and to the ultimate texture of the sauerkraut. Transfer the mixture to a clean 3-gallon (12-liter) stoneware crock and pound with a wooden kraut stomper to pack tightly.

Repeat the mixing and packing process two more times, until all the ingredients are used and the crock is three-quarters full. Place a china or stoneware plate upside-down on top of the vegetable mixture and press down, then add a heavy weight (such as a clean jar full of water, at least 4 pounds/2kg) on top of the plate. Once the vegetable mixture is weighed down, pour over enough spring water to completely submerge the china dish.

Cover the crock with cloth and stand in a warm room for 1 to 2 weeks, until the mixture begins to undergo an enzyme change—your nose will tell you because it will begin to smell like sauerkraut. At this point, relocate the crock to a cool, dark place and let the fermentation continue slowly for at least 1 month.

After 1 month, taste the sauerkraut. If you like the results, pack the mixture and some of the liquid into zip-top freezer bags, date and label, and freeze until needed. If the vegetables seem a little raw, continue fermentation for another week, or until you are happier with the outcome. Rather than freezing it to keep it good for several years, you can simply put it in jars in the refrigerator or in a cold room, cover, and dip into it as needed. It will last that way for more than a year; furthermore, you can eat this kraut mixture raw, but the flavor and texture are greatly improved by cooking for 25 to 30 minutes in a saucepan over medium heat.

Ten-Day Sauerkraut

This ingenious and uncomplicated recipe came to my attention while traveling in southern Poland many years ago. For the home cook anxious to produce a batch of sauerkraut quickly (as opposed to a three-month wait), here is the ideal shortcut. The addition of potato water provides food for the microbes doing the work of fermentation. In short, it kick-starts the process and then hastens it along. Similar results can be obtained by adding a little sourdough starter. Poverty under the Communist regime gave birth to recipes like this. Keep it as insurance for hard times.

Yield: About 3 pounds (1.5kg)

3 pounds (1.5kg) finely shredded cabbage

2½ tablespoons (38g) kosher sea salt

1 pound (500g) potatoes, pared and quartered (depending on intended future use)

1½ quarts (1.5 liters) spring water

With your hands, combine the shredded cabbage and salt in a deep work bowl, squeezing vigorously so that the cabbage is slightly bruised and limp; this bruising action is important to the fermentation process and to the ultimate texture of the sauerkraut. Transfer the mixture to a colander set in a large nonreactive bowl and drain at room temperature for at least 8 hours or overnight (do not discard the liquid). The next day, pack the drained cabbage tightly into a clean stoneware crock and pour the cabbage water over it.

In a large saucepan, combine the potatoes with 1½ quarts (1.5 liters) spring water and bring to a boil over medium-high heat. Boil until the potatoes are tender (about 25 minutes), then drain and reserve the potatoes for another use, also reserving the cooking water. Pour the starchy potato-cooking water over the cabbage. Cover the crock with a cloth and set aside in the kitchen to ferment for about 3 days. Once fermentation begins (your nose will tell you because it will smell like sauerkraut), place a china or stoneware plate upside-down on top of the cabbage mixture and top with a heavy weight (such as a clean jar full of water). Move the crock to a cool, dark spot and let ferment for 1 week, then transfer to freezer bags for later use or cook immediately like common sauerkraut. You can also store it in the refrigerator for up to 6 months, but it does not have the longer-keeping qualities of slowly fermented saurkraut. The best course is to consume it shortly after making it because you can replace it relatively quickly with a fresh batch.

Lebanese-Style Pickled Eggplant

I first encountered this delicious recipe in a restaurant in Limassol, Cyprus. The owner was fascinated with my research on medieval Cypriot cooking, and once we began talking recipes, my table was soon covered with all sorts of unique family dishes. This one stood out because it offers yet another creative way to deal with eggplants, not to mention that the pickle makes a terrific side dish for meze. For the gardener, Astrakom, Diamond, Little Finger, and Syrian stuffing eggplants are perfect for this recipe and are available from the Baker Creek Heirloom Seeds (see Sources, page 199). Their small size is important for avoiding the seediness of larger fruit, and the black skin turns bright purple, giving the marinade its trademark hue.

Yield: 2 quarts (2 liters)

3 pounds (1.5kg) small, long black eggplants

¼ cup (60g) kosher sea salt, plus for more seasoning

2¼ cups (565ml) red wine vinegar, divided

1 cup (125g) finely diced green bell pepper

½ cup (65g) finely diced sweet red pepper

2 teaspoons finely minced hot pepper, or to taste

½ cup (10g) coarsely chopped fresh parsley

¼ cup (10g) coarsely chopped fresh spearmint

4 garlic cloves, minced

1 cup (250ml) olive oil, plus at least ¼ cup (60ml) more for the jar

Julienne the eggplant into thin 1- to 2-inch-long (2.5- to 7.5-cm) slices, then lay in a colander set over a large bowl and toss with the salt. Cover with a plate and top with a weight. Let the eggplant drain at room temperature for 1 hour, then squeeze to wring out as much liquid as possible; do not rinse the eggplant. As the eggplant drains, sterilize the jar(s), lid(s), and ring(s) in a saucepan of lightly boiling water.

Place the drained eggplant in a deep nonreactive preserving pan with 1-quart (1 liter) spring water and 2 cups (500ml) of the vinegar. Set the heat to medium-high and bring the eggplant to a rolling boil (it should start to steam), then turn off the heat and let cool. Once cooled, drain off the liquid and squeeze or press the eggplant to release as much excess liquid as possible. Transfer the eggplant to a deep work bowl.

Add the green, red, and hot peppers, the parsley, mint, garlic, 1 cup (250ml) of the oil, and the remaining ¼ cup (65ml) vinegar. Stir well, taste, and adjust the seasonings, then pour into the prepared jar(s) and press the mixture down so that there are no air spaces. Add oil to cover the mixture by about ½ inch (1.25cm)—you may need more than ¼ cup (60ml) if you are using more than one jar. Cover with a tight-fitting lid and allow the mixture to marinate in the refrigerator for 1 month before serving (no further processing is needed). Let the pickled eggplant come to room temperature before serving.

While this pickle contains raw ingredients, it will keep for up to 6 months under refrigeration; however, in application it is more like a sandwich spread and is best made in fresh batches every few months.

Pickled-Salted *Huacatay* (*Condimento de Huacatay*)

Under the recipe for *Aji de Huacatay* (page 34), I have provided some background on this important Andean culinary herb. Since *huacatay*-flavored vinegar is suggested for the Peruvian Miscuchu Marinade (page 93), here is a spicy way to repurpose the by-products of making that vinegar: The *huacatay* leaves used to infuse the vinegar can then be converted into a condiment for poultry, meat, shellfish, or even plain baked potatoes. The salt-and-herb paste can also be applied to meats and poultry while grilling. If you happen to have more pickled *huacatay*, scale up the other ingredients accordingly to make a larger batch.

Yield: ¾ cup (180ml)

½ cup (50g) minced strained *huacatay* leaves from Huacatay Vinegar (page 194)

½ cup (15g) finely minced fresh parsley

2 tablespoons (5g) minced fresh spearmint

1 tablespoon (2.5g) minced fresh rosemary

2 garlic cloves, minced

1 tablespoon (15g) kosher sea salt

¼ cup (60ml) Huacatay Vinegar (page 194)

¼ cup (60ml) olive oil

1 teaspoon hot pepper powder, or to taste

1 tablespoon achiote powder (for grilling), optional

Thoroughly mix all the ingredients in a deep work bowl, then pack tightly into a clean, wide-mouthed jar, cover with a tight-fitting lid, and refrigerate (no further processing is needed). Do not keep this for longer than 6 months; after that the flavors will fade. If using the paste for grilling, add the achiote powder just before spreading it on the meat; if you're not grilling, no need to add achiote.

Polish-Style Cucumber Pickles

WhileI was visiting a farmstead near Nowy Sącz, Poland, this pickle was brought to the dinner table. My hosts had made it in a large barrel, and after inquiring about the recipe, I was surprised to find out how easy it was to prepare. I have reduced the original recipe for small-batch convenience, but you can double or quadruple the measurements without making further adjustments. In fact, this is one of those recipes best prepared in a large crock because you will find yourself dipping into it every day. To give this pickle some extra kick, try replacing half the volume of distilled white vinegar with homemade Horseradish Vinegar (page 194).

Yield: 2 quarts (2 liters)

2½ pounds (1.25kg) small pickling cucumbers

3½ tablespoons (55g) kosher sea salt, divided

½ medium carrot (about 2 ounces/60g)

½ cup (75g) pared and diced fresh horseradish, or to taste

16 pearl onions or small white onions, trimmed and peeled

1 tablespoon (10g) yellow mustard seeds

1 tablespoon (5g) whole coriander seeds

10 whole allspice berries

4 whole cloves

4 fresh bay leaves

1 large bunch fresh dill (15g)

5 cups (1.25 liters) distilled white vinegar (see headnote)

½ cup (125g) organic sugar

Trim and cut the cucumbers into 2-inch (5-cm) segments. Place them in a large clean jar. In a large nonreactive preserving pan, bring 2 quarts (2 liters) spring water to a rolling boil and add 2 tablespoons (30g) of the salt. Pour the brine over the cucumbers, cover with the lid, and let stand at room temperature overnight. The next day, pour off the brine and transfer the cucumbers to a large work bowl. Slice the carrot into thin coins and add to the cucumbers along with the horseradish and pearl onions.

Sterilize the jar(s), lid(s), and ring(s) in a saucepan of lightly boiling water. Combine the mustard seeds, coriander seeds, allspice, cloves, bay leaves, and dill in the prepared jar and add the vegetables.

Rinse the preserving pan and combine the vinegar (or vinegars; see headnote), the remaining 1½ tablespoons (25g) salt, the sugar, and 1 cup (250ml) spring water in the pan and bring to a rolling boil over medium-high heat. Pour the hot brine over the vegetables and cover with loose-fitting lid(s) (no further processing is needed). Store in a cool, dark place or in the refrigerator. Allow the pickles to mature for 3 weeks before using. This pickle will keep for more than 1 year, but is best consumed within 9 months.

Sadie Kriebel's Dill Tomatoes

As a counterpoint to the previous Polish recipe, here is an old-time crock pickle from the Pennsylvania Dutch Country made famous by the inimitable Sadie Krauss Kriebel (1906–1998). Sadie was a Schwenkfelder farmer from Palm, Pennsylvania, who for many years enlivened the traditional cooking demonstrations at the Kutztown Folk Festival. Hundreds of thousands of people got to know her and her colorful personality. Sadie is also well known among heirloom seed savers for single-handedly saving a rare lima bean from extinction (seeds are available from Roughwood; see Sources, page 199). Sadie's lima can be added to this pickle, and, since it retains its eye-catching reddish-black pattern when cooked, I also use it in Pickled Purslane with Limas (page 162). While you can make this recipe in a crock as Sadie did, I have adapted it to canning jars.

Yield: About 5 pints (2.5 liters)—I usually use five 1-pint (500-ml) jars

1 large bunch (15g) fresh dill

10 garlic cloves, thinly sliced lengthwise

½ red bell pepper (1 ½ ounces/45g), cut into short thin strips

2 pounds (1kg) small green cherry tomatoes or plum tomatoes, halved lengthwise

2½ teaspoons whole pink peppercorns

2½ teaspoons whole white peppercorns

5 teaspoons whole dill seeds

Five 3-inch (7.5-cm) slices fresh horseradish (sliced lengthwise)

¾ cup (180ml) distilled white vinegar

¼ cup (60g) kosher sea salt

Sterilize the jar(s), lid(s), and ring(s) in a saucepan of lightly boiling water.

Place several sprigs of fresh dill on the bottom of each prepared jar, then add 2 slices of garlic and 1 or 2 strips of red pepper. Fill each jar half full with tomatoes, then add ½ teaspoon each of the pink and white peppercorns and 1 teaspoon of the dill seeds. Add a few more strips of red pepper and 1 slice of horseradish to each. Fill with the remaining tomatoes and add a few more sprigs of dill and 2 more slices of garlic (be generous with the fresh dill—Sadie said you cannot add too much) to the top of each. If not using 5 small jars, simply divide the ingredients evenly for consistent results.

In a large nonreactive preserving pan, combine 5 cups (1.25 liters) spring water, the vinegar, and salt. Bring to a rolling boil over medium-high heat and boil for 4 minutes. Pour the boiling brine over the tomatoes and seal (see page 17). If you prefer the water bath method, allow 20 minutes.

Store in a cool, dark place; allow the pickle to mature for at least 3 weeks before opening. The tomatoes will keep for up to 2 years, but are best consumed within 9 months.

Salt-Cured Herbs

Traditional French Canadian cookery has its *herbes salées* for spicing soups and other dishes; so, too, have the Poles, who developed their own special formulas tracing back to medieval cookery and the need for flavoring food during periods of Lenten fasting. Convenience and easy storing have ensured that salted herb mixtures, known as *zasolone rośliny*, remain a cornerstone of a well-stocked Polish kitchen. The predominant flavor should be dill and parsley, although the lovage should not be downplayed. Bear garlic (*Allium ursinum*) is common in Polish forests; it is harvested in the spring and is often used as a condiment with game. Its North American counterpart is summertime ramps (*Allium tricoccum*), which make a good substitute. The root parsley called for is often sold as Berlin or Hamburg parsley; the greens can be used just like Italian flat-leaf parsley, while the white root has a flavor similar to parsnip (which can be used here as a substitute).

Yield: 1 quart (1 liter)

1½ cups (200g) finely minced root parsley (or parsnip)

1½ cups (90g) finely minced parsley (leaves only)

1½ cups (90g) finely minced fresh dill

1 cup (60g) finely minced lovage (leaves only)

½ cup (80g) minced leek, white part only

½ cup (50g) minced garlic chives or bear garlic (see headnote)

¼ cup (15g) finely minced fresh winter savory or thyme

1 tablespoon (5g) minced fresh rosemary

1 tablespoon (5g) ground coriander

2 teaspoons ground caraway

¾ cup (185g) kosher sea salt

Combine the root parsley, parsley leaves, dill, lovage, leek, garlic chives, winter savory, rosemary, coriander, and caraway in a deep work bowl, then add the salt and stir to mix thoroughly. Transfer the mixture to a clean wide-mouthed jar and close the lid tightly (no further processing is needed). Set in the refrigerator to infuse for at least 1 week before using. This will keep for more than a year in the refrigerator, even after opening.

Salt-Cured Shiso Blossoms

The flowers of green *shiso*, also known as perilla, make an excellent and highly flavorful garnish for all sorts of foods, even in sandwiches. The traditional Japanese salting technique is easy—all you need is a little patience! Harvest *shiso* flowers in the fall, when the heads are in full bloom and covered with tiny white blossoms—use the entire flower head. You can soak the flowers in fresh water to remove some of the saltiness, in which case just pat the blossoms dry with a towel and use as desired.

Yield: About 100 salt-cured *shiso* blossoms

3 cups (725) kosher sea salt, divided

100 *shiso* (perilla) blossoms, trimmed from hard stems

Line a 10-inch (25-cm) square glass baking pan with a double layer of paper towels. Cover the bottom of the pan with 2 cups (500g) of the salt. Lay the flower heads side by side on the salt, pressing down slightly so that they are half buried. Once all are in the salt, scatter the remaining 1 cup (225g) salt over the top to cover the blossoms fully.

Set the pan in a cool, dry place to rest overnight, then transfer the blossoms and salt into a large wide-mouthed canning jar, placing the flowers and salt in alternating layers. Cover and store in a cool, dark pantry. After about 1 month, the flowers will be completely desiccated and brown in color. They are ready to use as condiments in soups—just shake off the salt. The salt-cured blossoms will keep for at least 2 years in a cool, dark place if stored in layers of salt in a plastic container.

Note: My friend Eri Domae, who is involved in the *shumei* (natural farming) movement in the United States, sent me a recipe that follows a different salting technique, one intended to reduce the amount of salt used, and technically wasted, in the recipe above. By this method, the *shiso* blossoms are first soaked overnight in fresh water, then the next day drained and patted dry between paper towels. The *shiso* heads are then mixed with about 35 percent of their weight in salt in a glass container and refrigerated as needed. It should be noted, however, that even after following the original salting technique, the used salt is perfectly good to use again in another pickling recipe once all the *shiso* has been removed.

Snippled Beans (Beankraut)

Beankraut (*Buhnegraut*) is another Pennsylvania Dutch preparation that deserves wider circulation among home cooks. The combination of cabbage, string beans, onions, and summer savory make this delightful version a must for anyone who enjoys high-end farmhouse fare. When cooked with smoked duck or ham dumplings, you will have a ready-made homestyle feast for the holidays. For best results, use a sterilized 3-gallon (12-liter) stoneware crock.

Yield: About 10 pounds (5 kilos)

7½ pounds (3.75kg) finely shredded white cabbage

3 pounds (1.5kg) thinly sliced onions

9 tablespoons (135g) kosher sea salt

3 pounds (1.5kg) "snippled" string beans (thinly sliced on the bias)

2¼ cups (135g) fresh summer savory, leaves stripped from the stems

18 garlic cloves, finely minced or squeezed through a garlic press

Divide each of the ingredients into three equal portions: You will fill the crock with three even layers of the combined ingredients. Once divided, combine 2½ pounds (1.25kg) cabbage, 1 pound (500g) sliced onion, and 3 tablespoons (45g) salt in a deep work bowl. Using your hands, squeeze the mixture vigorously so the ingredients are lightly bruised to facilitate the fermentation process and ultimate texture of the beankraut. Add 1 pound (500g) snippled beans, ¾ cup (60g) savory leaves, and 6 minced or pressed garlic cloves, mixing well with your hands. Transfer the mixture to a clean 3-gallon (12-liter) stoneware crock and pound with a wooden kraut stomper to pack the ingredients as tightly as possible.

Repeat the mixing and packing process two more times, until all the ingredients are used and the crock is three-quarters full. Place a china or stoneware plate upside-down on top of the vegetable mixture and press down, then add a heavy weight (such as a clean jar full of water, at least 4 pounds/2kg) on top of the plate. Once the vegetable mixture is weighed down, pour over enough spring water to completely submerge the china dish.

Cover the crock with cloth and let it stand in a warm room for 1 to 2 weeks, until the mixture begins to undergo an enzyme change—your nose will tell you because it will smell like sauerkraut. At this point, relocate the crock to a cool, dark place and let the fermentation continue slowly for at least 1 month.

After 1 month, taste the beankraut. If you like the results, pack the mixture and some of the liquid into zip-top freezer bags, date and label, and freeze until needed. If the vegetables seem a little raw, continue fermentation for another week, or until you are happier with the outcome. You can also store it in jars in the refrigerator or in a cold room for up to 6 months.

While you can eat the snippled beans uncooked like a salad, it is intensely flavored and somewhat raw until cooked over medium heat for at least 30 minutes. This not only tenderizes the vegetables but also mellows the flavors, especially when cooked with ham or sausages.

Sproutkraut (Brussels Sprouts Sauerkraut)

This is a very straightforward recipe with many delicious applications. Served uncooked, it makes a simple side dish. Cooked like sauerkraut, it goes beautifully alongside savory roasts like smoked ham—try cooking the sproutkraut with chopped apples and sprinkle with crispy slab bacon. You can freeze it, which also effectively tenderizes the sprouts; however, frozen sproutkraut can only then be cooked before serving. You can also can the fermented sprouts in jars with dill and lemon zest as a brightly flavored pickle. For best results, use a sanitized 3-gallon (12-liter) stoneware crock.

Yield: About 7½ pounds (Approximately 3½ kg)

7½ pounds (approximately 3½ kg) thinly sliced Brussels sprouts (sliced through root end)

6½ tablespoons (95g) kosher sea salt, divided

In a large work bowl, combine the sliced Brussels sprouts with 4½ tablespoons (68g) of the salt, mixing thoroughly with your hands. Transfer to a clean 3-gallon (12-liter) crock and pack tightly so that the crock is about three-quarters full, pressing down on the mixture. Place a china or stoneware plate upside-down on top of the mixture, then add a heavy weight (such as a clean jar full of water, at least 4 pounds/2kg) on top of the plate. Once the vegetable mixture is weighed down, pour over enough spring water to completely submerge the china dish. Add the remaining 2 tablespoons (27g) salt and cover the crock with a cloth.

Stand the crock in a warm room for 1 to 2 weeks, until the mixture begins to undergo an enzyme change—your nose will tell you because it will smell like sauerkraut. Taste the sproutkraut, and if it is too sour, add a little more salt. After two weeks, relocate the crock to a cool, dark place and let the fermentation continue slowly for at least 1 month or longer to achieve your desired flavor; the longer the sprouts ferment, the more they are tenderized by the process.

Drain the sprouts, discarding the liquid, and serve or freeze in gallon-storage bags for later use.

Syrian-Style Brined Beets and Cauliflower

This pickle technique is used for brining sheep and goat tongues, but it works just as well with these vegetables (which also go into the tongue pickles). The garlic flavor is very pleasant and makes this an ideal pickle for meze. A squeeze of fresh lemon over the pickles right before serving will add zip to their flavor.

Yield: 2 quarts (2 liters)

4 large beets, peeled and quartered

1 cup (250ml) red wine vinegar

¼ cup (60g) kosher sea salt

1 pound (500g) freshly picked cauliflower, core removed and broken into florets (weight after coring)

8 large garlic cloves, halved lengthwise

In a large nonreactive preserving pan, combine the quartered beets with 2 quarts (2 liters) spring water. Cook over medium heat until the beets are tender and easily pierced with a skewer, about 30 minutes. Remove the beets, reserving 5 cups (1.25 liters) of the cooking liquid (now, beet stock), and set aside. While the beets cook, sterilize a 2-quart (2-liter) wide-mouthed canning jar, lid, and ring in a saucepan of lightly boiling water.

Add the reserved beet stock, the vinegar and salt in the preserving pan and place over medium heat. While the brine is heating, slice the reserved beets and transfer them to the bottom of the prepared jar, then add a layer of cauliflower florets and half of the garlic. Add more beets, garlic, and cauliflower, and continue until the jar is full, finishing with sliced beets on top.

Once the pickling brine comes to a full rolling boil, pour it over the vegetable mixture and cover with a lid (do not microwave seal). Once cooled, refrigerate for at least 2 weeks before opening. The brined beets will keep for at least 6 months in the refrigerator.

03

Sweet and Sour

Southeastern Pennsylvania is one of the richest areas in the United States for culinary biodiversity and the third largest producer of food in the country, yet our three hundred-year-old gardens-based cuisine is still underrated. Since I live in close proximity to some of the best traditional cooks in the Pennsylvania Dutch region (comprising some twenty-five counties), it is no surprise that I have tipped honors in their direction. Beet *schnittles*, corn relish, Pottsville pickle, scrapple sauce, sweet and sour plums, and vinegar cherries are only a few of the regional classics that still grace the pantries of local kitchens. This is the food I grew up on.

On that note, I also doff my hat in the direction of my great-grandmother, Esther Hannum Hickman, whose pickling expertise became a family tradition. Her Cassia Pickle (page126), Five-Bean Chow-Chow (page 128), Gooseberry Chutney (page 129), Green Tomato Catsup (page 130), and Green Tomato Mincemeat (page 132) are heirloom recipes that I am proud to include here. I used to barter Esther's recipes during my traveling days in the Italian Veneto. A maid at the Hotel Villa Cipriani in Asolo traded the head chef's family recipe for Venetian Pumpkin Mostarda (page 187) for Esther's pineapple upside-down cake. Believe it or not, that cake was served at an Asolo wedding and all present were agog that the pineapple came out of tins from an American airbase. Had the catering staff dressed as cowboys, this all-American fantasy in the foothills of the Alps would have been complete.

As spiritual salve, I often dip (glass of champagne in hand) into old French cookbooks. The impeccable treatment of ingredients is unmistakable, and no matter what their age, I find the recipes highly inspiring. This is why you will find a classic 1809 recipe for fragrant spring vinegar, *Vinaigre Printanier*, on page 189. It is one of my favorites, and anyway, herb-flavored vinegars should be part of any pickle cook's repertoire. If they are as elegant and as complex as this one, they can make delicate pickles even better. Designed to enhance spring salads, no bottled dressing will compare. It condenses into one recipe a basic culinary course on the meaning of flavor.

Beet *Schnittles*

Sweet-and-sour beet *schnittle* (pronounced *SHNITT-lay*) are considered one of the classic beet pickles from the Pennsylvania Dutch Country. This is also the basic pickling brine for red hard-cooked eggs—beets, not food coloring, are what make the real thing that eye-popping color. (Shelled hard-boiled eggs may be added to the pickle, but if doing so, use a large glass container and pour the hot brine over the beets and eggs; marinate the eggs separately for five days under refrigeration, then use with the beets as needed.) Early Blood Turnip beet and Bull's Blood beet are the only heirloom beet varieties that will yield the kind of color and texture that live up to the old-time *schnittle* reputation. The secret ingredient, however, is the raspberry vinegar—the fruitiness of raspberries balances the earthiness some people dislike in beets. The Dutch Touch comes with the cassia, which is cinnamon-plus, if I may describe it that way. A bit on the spicy side, cassia conveys a lost flavor from early Pennsylvania farmhouse cookery.

Yield: 2 quarts (2 liters)

2½ pounds (1.25kg) heirloom red beets

½ teaspoon whole cassia buds (or 4 cinnamon sticks), optional

3 cups (750ml) Raspberry Vinegar (page 197)

1 cup (250g) organic sugar

1½ teaspoons kosher sea salt

Sterilize jar(s), lid(s), and ring(s) in a saucepan of lightly boiling water.

In a large nonreactive preserving pan, combine the beets with enough cold water to cover them by at least 1 inch (2.5cm), then bring to a simmer over medium heat. Cook gently until tender, about 30 minutes. Measure and set aside 1 cup (250ml) of the beet stock; the rest may be used for making beet soup or for pickling eggs.

Run the cooked beets under cold water to loosen the skins, then peel them off with your hands or a vegetable peeler. Slice the beets into thin strips (schnittle), then transfer to the prepared jar(s). Add the cassia, if using.

In a large saucepan, combine the vinegar, sugar, salt, and the reserved beet broth. Place over high heat, bring to a hard, rolling boil, and boil for 3 minutes. Pour this over the beets and seal by placing the jars upside-down once the lids are tightly screwed down. There is no need to microwave this pickle because it is stable at ambient temperatures, but if you prefer a water bath, give the beets at least 10 minutes. Store in a cool, dry place out of direct sunlight, where it will keep for up to 6 months.

Apple Chutney

This Indian-style chutney was originally intended to make use of fallen green apples, a practical and delicious way to recycle produce that might otherwise go wasted. If you have an apple tree and wonder what to do with those apples brought down by a storm, here is the perfect solution. Otherwise, you can use Granny Smith or any under ripe crisp apple. Fortunately, the spices can make up for any shortcomings in the fruit, and the complex flavors are perfect with grilled meats and vegetables. Because this chutney is muddy brown, some Indian cooks add sandalwood to create a brick-red color, which will not alter the taste—this is not the same tree used for sandalwood incense.

Yield: 2 quarts (2 liters)

¼ cup (60ml) virgin (cold-pressed) sesame oil or almond oil

1 tablespoon (10g) whole anise seeds

1 tablespoon (10g) whole cumin seeds

1 tablespoon (10g) black mustard seeds

3 pounds (1.5kg) pared and cored tart green cooking apples or unripe apples (weight after paring and coring)

2 tablespoons (50g) freshly grated ginger

2 tablespoons (50g) minced garlic

1½ tablespoons (8g) hot chile powder, or to taste

1 tablespoon (15g) kosher sea salt

1½ cups (375g) organic sugar

1¼ cups (315ml) apple cider vinegar

2 tablespoons (10g) culinary sandalwood, optional

Sterilize the jar(s), lid(s), and ring(s) in a saucepan of lightly boiling water.

In a heavy sauté pan, combine the oil and anise, cumin, and mustard seeds. Place over high heat and cook until the seeds begin to crackle and pop. Remove from the heat, then strain the toasted seeds and transfer to a mortar, reserving the oil. Gently crush the toasted seeds into coarse pieces.

Weigh the prepared fruit to be certain you have 3 pounds (1.5kg) and quarter the apples. Shred the apples in a food processor or against the large holes of a vegetable grater and place in a large nonreactive preserving pan. Add the reserved oil, the crushed anise, cumin, and mustard seeds, the ginger, garlic, chile powder, salt, sugar, and vinegar. Place over medium heat, bring to a simmer, and cook for 40 to 45 minutes, stirring frequently. Once the chutney thickens, add the sandalwood, if using, then remove from the heat and ladle into the prepared jar(s) and seal (see page 17). You can use the chutney immediately or store it in a cool place for more than 2 years. It will keep for up to 4 months in the refrigerator after opening.

Corn Relish

This was one of my grandmother's favorite recipes, a classic Pennsylvania Dutch pickle utilizing field-fresh sweet corn. If your corn is more than a day old, poach it for fivr minutes in boiling water *before* removing the kernels. Repurpose spent cobs by boiling them in the poaching water to make a flavorful vegan stock for soup.

Yield: 3 quarts (3 liters)

6 cups (900g) corn kernels, cut from the cobs (about 8 fresh ears)

4 cups (500g) chopped cabbage

3 cups (500g) chopped onion

½ cup (75g) finely diced sweet red pepper

2 cups (300g) finely diced green bell pepper

1 tablespoon (10g) whole celery seeds

1 teaspoon ground turmeric

1½ tablespoons (15g) yellow mustard seeds

1½ cups (375g) organic sugar

3 cups (750ml) white wine vinegar or Garlic Vinegar (page 194)

1½ tablespoons (25g) kosher sea salt, or to taste

2 tablespoons (10g) Korean chile flakes *(gochugaru)*, optional

Sterilize the jar(s), lid(s), and ring(s) in a saucepan of lightly boiling water.

In a deep nonreactive preserving pan, combine the corn, cabbage, onion, red and green pepper, celery seeds, turmeric, mustard seeds, sugar, vinegar, and salt. Bring to a gentle boil over medium heat and cook for 40 minutes. If you prefer the relish spicy, add the chile flakes, stir well, then pour the relish into the prepared jar(s) and seal (see page 17). Store in a cool, dark place for up to 2 years, but the relish is best when used within 9 months.

Dilled Baby Asparagus

While there is nothing to compare with fresh asparagus, for asparagus lovers, this pickle is perhaps the most practical way to enjoy the vegetable year-round, although in flavor the pickle resembles French cornichons. For this reason, these are best in salads, as garnishes to hearty dishes, or served with cheese and beer. The only downside is that asparagus gets wrinkly when pickled and the colors fade—violet turns pink and the green ones go pale, but happily the blanched (white) spears stay white. In spite of their higher cost, blanched spears are probably the best choice for this type of recipe, but you be the judge. Regardless, the mixed pickle is quite an ornament for holiday dinners when fresh asparagus is out of season.

Yield: 2 quarts (2 liters)

60 to 75 young, thin spears of asparagus (use mixed colors: green, violet, blanched)

⅓ cup (90g) plus 2 tablespoons (30g) kosher sea salt, divided

1 tablespoon (10g) yellow mustard seeds

1 tablespoon (10g) whole dill seeds

6 fresh bay leaves

1 medium onion (about 8 ounces/125g), cut in half lengthwise, then thinly sliced

¼ cup (45g) minced hot red pepper

1 large bunch fresh dill (about 15g), plus a few dill flowers

1½ tablespoons (8g) fresh thyme leaves (from about 6 large sprigs)

3 cups (750ml) white wine vinegar

⅔ cup (155g) organic sugar

Sterilize the jar(s), lid(s), and ring(s) in a saucepan of lightly boiling water.

Trim the asparagus to a length of about 6 inches (15cm). In a large work bowl, combine the asparagus with ⅓ cup (90g) of the salt dissolved in 2 quarts (2 liters) water. Let sit for 2 hours to marinate, then drain, rinse the asparagus under cold water, and pat dry.

Combine the mustard seeds, dill seeds, bay leaves, onion, hot pepper, dill greens, and thyme leaves in the prepared jar. Carefully pack the asparagus standing on end—tips up—making certain to arrange them in alternating colors.

In a large nonreactive preserving pan, combine the vinegar, sugar, the remaining 2 tablespoons (30g) salt, and 3 cups (750ml) spring water. Bring to a rolling boil over medium heat, boil for 2 minutes, then pour the brine over the asparagus and seal (see page 17). Store in a cool, dark place, where it will keep for 2 years; for best results, make each spring when young asparagus comes in season.

Esther Hickman's Cassia Pickle

While I am not too fond of overly sweet pickles, this is one of those classic old Philadelphia recipes taught in Sarah Tyson Rorer's cooking school, and thus variations can be found in many local heirloom cookbooks. My great-grandmother, Esther Hannum Hickman, studied at Mrs. Rorer's school in the 1880s and developed this one. I first tested her recipe in 1987 under the cautionary eye of my grandmother, who hadn't made it since the 1940s. For those who abjure hot peppers, there is nary a one in this recipe. In place of heat, cassia buds in tandem with ginger, allspice, and cloves contribute warm, spicy flavors. Leftover liquid from the pickle can be used in vinaigrettes—try it in a hot bacon dressing served over wilted lettuce or cabbage—and it is also excellent spooned over cooked beets.

Yield: 4 quarts (4 liters)

4 pounds (2kg) small green tomatoes, cored and thinly sliced

6 tablespoons (90g) kosher sea salt, divided

About 1 pound (500g) small-diced sweet red peppers (2 whole peppers)

2 whole limes, finely minced (including peel and pith; seeds discarded)

1 pound (500g) onions, cut in half lengthwise, then thinly sliced

1 cup (200g) diced celery

½ cup (100g) diced carrot

¼ cup (20g) powdered mustard

¼ cup (40g) yellow mustard seeds

2 tablespoons (50g) freshly grated ginger

2 tablespoons (30g) whole cassia buds

1 tablespoon (10g) whole celery seeds

2 teaspoons ground allspice

1 teaspoon ground cloves

3½ cups (875g) organic sugar

7 cups (1.65 liters) distilled white vinegar

Sterilize the jar(s), lid(s), and ring(s) in a saucepan of lightly boiling water.

In a colander set over a large bowl, toss the tomatoes with 4 tablespoons (60g) of the salt. Cover and let stand overnight at room temperature to drain. The next day, discard the liquid but do not rinse the tomatoes. Transfer the tomatoes to a deep nonreactive preserving pan and add the sweet peppers, limes, onion, celery, carrot, powdered mustard, mustard seeds, ginger, cassia buds, celery seeds, allspice, cloves, sugar, and vinegar. Place over medium heat, bring to a gentle boil, and cook for 25 minutes. Taste and adjust the seasoning, adding salt 1 tablespoon (15g) at a time, depending on the acidity of the tomatoes.

Transfer the pickle to the prepared jar(s) and seal (see page 17). If using the water bath method, allow 10 minutes. Let the pickle mature for 1 month before using. This recipe keeps well for up to 3 years in a cool, dark place, but is best when consumed within 1 year.

Five-Bean Chow-Chow

This is another recipe from my great-grandmother, but with some twists of my own. For best visual results, use small wide-mouthed jars. In larger jars, the white beans tend to settle to the bottom or everything rises to the top, leaving too much space at the bottom.

Yield: 6½ quarts (6.5 liters)—I usually use twenty-six 1-pint (500-ml) jars

2 quarts (800g) yellow string beans

2 quarts (800g) green string beans

1 quart (600g) shelled lima beans

½ quart (250g) green shelly beans or edamame

1 quart (800g) marrowfat beans or cannellini beans

2 cups (250g) diced sweet red pepper

2 cups (150g) thinly sliced or diced celery (4 stalks)

7 tablespoons (70g) whole celery seeds

5 tablespoons (50g) yellow mustard seeds

6 cups (1.5kg) organic sugar

6 cups (1.5 liters) cider vinegar

6 tablespoons (90g) kosher sea salt

Sterilize the jar(s), lid(s), and ring(s) in a saucepan of lightly boiling water and set aside.

Trim and cut the yellow and green string beans into different shapes—for example, cut the yellow string beans into blunt ½-inch (1.25-cm) segments, then snipple the green ones diagonally (this is purely for textural and visual contrast; if you prefer the beans the same size and shape, that's fine).

Fill a large nonreactive preserving pan with water and bring to a rolling boil over medium-high heat. Add the trimmed string beans and poach for exactly 5 minutes to tenderize them, then remove the string beans from the water with a strainer (keep it at a boil), shock in cold running water, and set aside. Add the lima beans and shelly beans and poach for exactly 5 minutes, then strain out and add to the string beans. Add the marrowfat beans and cook until tender but not soft, 20 to 25 minutes. Strain and add them to the bean mixture, then discard the water.

Add the sweet red pepper and celery to the poached beans. Mix the celery seeds and mustard seeds in a small bowl and distribute evenly between the prepared jars. Pack the bean mixture into the jars.

Combine the sugar, vinegar, salt, and 2 cups (500ml) spring water in the now-empty preserving pan and bring to a rolling boil. Boil for about 3 minutes, then pour the brine over the bean mixture in the jars and seal (see page 17). Let the chow-chow mature for 3 weeks before using. It will keep for at least 2 years in a cool, dark cupboard.

Gooseberry Chutney

My great-grandmother often served this chutney with *bobotie*, little curried venison cakes that were once a popular hors d'oeuvre served at hunt luncheons. If you aren't the hunt-luncheon type, this chutney is also delicious with any curried meat. Two alternate preparations to the method below will yield distinctly different textures: For a smooth, sauce-like consistency, add the raisins then puree the chutney before sealing; for a little more bite, puree the cooked gooseberry mixture until smooth, then reheat and add the raisins before sealing.

Yield: About 7 cups (1.75 liters)

1½ pounds (750g) fresh gooseberries

1 medium onion (8 ounces/250g), finely chopped

3 tablespoons (75g) minced garlic

2 tablespoons (50g) freshly grated ginger

2 tablespoons (20g) yellow mustard seeds, coarsely crushed in a mortar and pestle

1½ tablespoons (25g) kosher sea salt

3 cups (750g) organic sugar

1 tablespoon (5g) hot Madras curry powder

1½ tablespoons (7g) hot chile powder, or to taste

½ cup (125ml) distilled white vinegar

1 cup (125g) green raisins (green sultanas or Thompson seedless green raisins)

Sterilize the jar(s), lid(s), and ring(s) in a saucepan of lightly boiling water and set aside.

Combine the gooseberries, onion, garlic, ginger, crushed mustard seeds, salt, sugar, curry powder, chile powder, and vinegar in a large nonreactive preserving pan. Set over medium heat and cook for 15 minutes, or until thick, then add the raisins and cook for another 10 minutes, or until the raisins are soft. Transfer to the prepared jars and seal (see page 17). This will keep for at least 2 years in a cool, dark place. Once opened, treat it like marmalade and use at once.

Green Tomato Catsup

Green tomato catsup was an old-time favorite in my great-grandmother's family because it normally was served with scrapple, one of the products of the Hickman butchering business. It is similarly excellent with breakfast sausage, ham croquettes, smoked pork chops, and even fried codfish balls. Its tangy flavor and heat are a real contrast to common red catsup (or ketchup), which is often overly sweet—this is why green tomato catsup pairs so well with smoked meats and even smoked fish.

Yield: 6 pints (3 liters)

4 pounds (2kg) green tomatoes, chopped

2 medium onions (1 pound/500g), chopped

4 jalapeño peppers, seeded (4 ounces/125g), or to taste (weight after seeding)

1 quart (1 liter) distilled white vinegar

2 cups (500g) organic sugar

2 tablespoons (10g) powdered mustard

½ teaspoon ground cloves

1 teaspoon ground allspice

2 tablespoons (10g) ground coriander

¼ cup (60g) kosher sea salt, plus more for seasoning

Sterilize the jar(s), lid(s), and ring(s) in a saucepan of lightly boiling water and set aside.

In a large nonreactive preserving pan, combine the tomatoes, onions, peppers, and vinegar and set over medium heat. Cook gently for 25 minutes, or until reduced to a soft mash. Transfer to a food processor or high-speed blender and process until smooth and creamy—be careful when pureeing hot mixtures.

Rinse the pan and return the pureed green tomato mixture to it and add the sugar, mustard, cloves, allspice, coriander, and salt. Place over medium-high heat and cook for 15 minutes, or until thickened as desired, then taste and adjust the seasoning, adding up to 2 tablespoons (30g) more salt, depending on the acidity of the tomatoes. Transfer to the prepared jars and seal (see page 17). This will keep for up to 3 years in a cool, dark place, but the flavors will begin to fade in the third year, so it's best consumed within the first 2 years.

Green Tomato Mincemeat

This completely vegetarian take on old-fashioned green tomato mincemeat will keep for more than a year when sealed in canning jars (it is really a chutney knockoff). Usually 1 pint (500ml) is sufficient for a 10-inch (25cm) pie, but if you prefer a thicker filling, add 1 tablespoon (5g) powdered agar-agar per pie before filling and baking. I prefer agar-agar to flour or egg yolks as a thickener because it yields a more even texture (it will slice like a lemon meringue pie, which means you can eliminate a top crust, traditional for mincemeat pies) and help to amplify the fruitiness of the tomatoes; also, it is vegetarian. Otherwise, go traditional and thicken your mincemeat with beef tallow, which at room temperature so resembles white wax you could even make candles from it. For a typical two-crusted mincemeat pie, baking time is typically 35 to 40 minutes at 375°F (190°C).

Yield: 3 pints (1.5 liters), enough for 3 mincemeat pies

2½ pounds (1.25kg) green tomatoes, cut into small dice

1 cup (200g) diced underripe mango

2 cups (315g) organic light brown sugar

2 tablespoons (30ml) honey

¼ cup (60ml) red wine vinegar

1 tablespoon (25g) freshly grated ginger

Grated zest and juice of 1 lime

1 tablespoon (5g) grated orange zest

⅛ teaspoon ground cloves

1 teaspoon ground mace

½ teaspoon ground star anise

1 tablespoon (15g) kosher sea salt, or to taste

1 cup (125g) coarsely chopped hickory nuts or walnuts

Sterilize the jar(s), ring(s), and lid(s) in a saucepan of lightly boiling water and set aside.

In a large nonreactive preserving pan, combine the tomatoes, mango, brown sugar, honey, vinegar, and ginger and cover. Set over medium heat and cook for 20 minutes, or until the mixture begins to thicken. Uncover and add the lime zest and juice, orange zest, cloves, mace, star anise, salt, and nuts and continue cooking for about 15 minutes, stirring from time to time, until thick and most of the liquid has evaporated. Transfer to the prepared jars and seal (see page 17). I have kept this for as long as 5 years without any decline in flavor, but I think it is best used within 1 year. Like other pickles it should be stored in a cool, dark place.

Japanese-Style Baby Okra with Seaweed

Pairing seaweed with okra comes from an old Japanese Buddhist tradition and initially may seem like a tough sell to Western palates. All the same, this authentic recipe will appeal to vegetarians looking for new flavor experiences. The marriage of slippery seaweed with soft and glutinous okra is unique, and when using kombu (which contains natural glutamate), the flavor is enhanced to the point that this pickle can be treated as a dish by itself. It needs nothing else unless you want to add a bowl of rice.

Regarding the *shiso* blossoms, you will need forty like those shown on page 110. Remove woody stems but keep the small leaves at the base. Tie the blossoms into small bouquets with kitchen twine or string—four blossoms to a bouquet, ten bouquets total.

Yield: 2½ quarts (2.5 liters)—I use five 1-pint (0.5-liter) jars

Eight 7½- to 8-inch (18- to 20-cm) strips kombu seaweed

2 pounds (1kg) fresh baby okra, stems and tips trimmed

4 large garlic cloves, quartered lengthwise

2 ounces (60g) fresh ginger, peeled and sliced into coins

1 medium onion (8 ounces/250g), cut in half lengthwise, then thinly sliced

15 to 20 long, thin hot red peppers, sliced into small rings with or without seeds, to taste

10 bouquets green shiso (perilla) blossoms (see headnote)

1½ cups (375ml) white balsamic vinegar

1½ cups (375ml) white wine vinegar

1½ cups (375ml) mirin

3 tablespoons (45g) kosher sea salt

Sterilize the jar(s), lid(s), and ring(s) in a saucepan of lightly boiling water and set aside.

In a large heatproof work bowl, pour 1 quart (1 liter) of boiling water over the kombu. Let sit for 45 minutes, or until soft. Remove from the soaking water, pat dry, and slice into ½-inch (1.25-cm) strips; reserve 2½ cups (625ml) of the soaking water. Transfer the kombu to a second work bowl and add the trimmed okra, the garlic, ginger, onion, and hot peppers.

Place 1 bouquet of *shiso* blossoms on the bottom of each prepared jar, then fill with the seaweed mixture. In a large nonreactive preserving pan, combine the white balsamic vinegar, white wine vinegar, reserved kombu soaking water, mirin, and salt. Bring to a rolling boil over medium-high heat. Place the remaining blossom bouquets on top of the seaweed and okra mixture (1 bouquet to a jar), then pour the hot brine over this and seal (see page 17). Store in a cool, dark place for up to 2 years, but the flavor and texture are best when used within 1 year.

Japanese-Style Sweet and Sour Plums

This excellent recipe pins its success on the quality and freshness of the plums. They should be firm and underripe, yet in full blush of color. Many are sold as "red plums," so choose carefully: The most authentic varieties are small and red-fleshed; others are larger with red skin, but the flesh is yellow, so they will not develop the rich color that makes this pickle so distinctive. Lacking the real thing, use any dark plum as long as the fruit is slightly underripe (the firmer the better). Large plums should be quartered or even sliced into eighths. The shiso, fresh ginger, and hot peppers contribute to this recipe's unique character, so increase them according to your taste and the type of fruit used. Serve the pickle at room temperature liberally garnished with finely minced spring onions, chives, or garlic chives. Any pickling brine remaining after the plums are eaten can be used as a marinade for poultry or pork.

Yield: 1½ quarts (1.5 liters)—I usually use 1 large wide-mouthed canning jar

2 cups (160g) red perilla (*shiso*) leaves, or more to taste (at least 60 leaves)

2 pounds (1kg) small red plums, halved and pitted (quartered if large)

Six 2-inch-long (5-cm) slices fresh ginger

1 small hot red pepper (or more depending on size), sliced into rings (at least ¼ cup/25g)

1 cup (250ml) white balsamic vinegar

1 cup (250ml) rice vinegar

¾ cup (190ml) mirin

½ cup (125g) organic sugar

2 tablespoons (30g) kosher sea salt

½ cup (125ml) high-grade sake

Sterilize the jar(s), lid(s), and ring(s) in a saucepan of lightly boiling water and set aside.

Divide half of the shiso between the prepared jar(s). Add the plums, ginger, and hot pepper, then pack the remaining shiso on top.

In a large nonreactive preserving pan, combine the white balsamic vinegar, rice vinegar, mirin, sugar, and salt. Place over medium-high heat and bring to a rolling boil. Boil for 3 minutes, then pour over the plums and add the sake. Seal (see page 17) and store in a dark, cool place, where it will keep for 6 months.

Pickled Truffles or Wild Mushrooms

It may seem inordinately extravagant to pickle truffles, but when you have them by the quart basket emerging from the garden and more readily available for the digging, such an overplus demands epicurean solutions. I took to putting them up in vinegar Polish-style, only to discover later that the recipe also worked for any kind of wild mushroom, especially *cèpes de Bordeaux* and porcini mushrooms or chicken of the woods (*Laetiporus sulphureus*), mainly because of their shared meaty texture. The recipe is rich and heavily spiced, so I put it up in small jars.

I have never attempted this recipe with black truffles, which probably would call for some adjustment in the spices, as the flavor of black truffles is more intense than that of white truffles. Should you prefer to enhance the truffle or mushroom flavor in this pickle, reduce or even eliminate the allspice, cut the salt and sugar in half, and replace half of the white wine vinegar with spring water or white wine. This milder brine will appeal to those who prefer the earthy taste of mushrooms—but do not leave out the fresh bay leaves.

Yield: 4 pints (2 liters)—I usually use four 1-pint (500-ml) jars

12 fresh bay leaves

2 teaspoons whole black peppercorns

4 teaspoons (35g) whole allspice berries

4 teaspoons (13g) yellow mustard seeds

1½ pounds (750g) white truffles or wild mushrooms, cleaned and trimmed

4 tablespoons (60g) kosher sea salt, divided

4 cups (1 liter) white wine vinegar

6 tablespoons (90g) organic sugar

Sterilize the jars, lids, and rings in a saucepan of lightly boiling water. Divide the bay leaves, peppercorns, allspice, and mustard evenly among the prepared jars.

Slice the truffles ¼ inch (6mm) thick, then into 2-inch (5-cm) lengths or bite-size pieces. In a large nonreactive preserving pan, dissolve 2 tablespoons (30g) of the salt in 2 quarts (2 liters) spring water. Set over medium-high heat and bring to a full rolling boil. Add the truffles and poach for about 8 minutes, then remove with a slotted spoon and transfer to the prepared jars.

Rinse the preserving pan, and combine the vinegar, the remaining 2 tablespoons (30g) salt, and the sugar in the pan with 1 cup (250ml) spring water. Set over medium-high heat, bring to a full rolling boil, and boil for 3 minutes, then pour the hot brine over the truffle mixture and seal (see page 17). Let the pickle mature in a cool, dark place for at least 3 weeks before using. The pickle will keep for at least 3 years but is best consumed within 9 months.

Philadelphia Pepper Hash

One of the great classics of American regional cookery, pepper hash was a popular side served with everything in old-time oyster houses, considered a must with catfish and waffles. In fact, this recipe traces to Mrs. Watkins's Old Catfish and Coffee House at the Falls of the Schuylkill River, an eatery famous in the mid-nineteenth century for its regional cuisine and woodsy location along the water.

While pepper hash was not created in Philadelphia—it was brought over from England as cabbage hash spiced with mustard—local cooks added the peppers, tinkered with the sweet-and-sour flavor, and more or less reinvented it as something unique to the region. Whether a muskrat dinner in South Jersey, a crab boil on the Maryland Eastern Shore, or a church social fried-chicken dinner, pepper hash was there. This pickle is best put up in small jars because you only need a small amount at any given meal.

Yield: About 2½ quarts (2.5 liters)—I usually use 6 or 7 small jars

One 3-pound (1.5-kg) head of cabbage

6 tablespoons (90g) kosher sea salt

3 medium green bell peppers

3 medium red bell peppers

4 jalapeño peppers (4 ounces/125g)

2½ cups (425g) finely chopped onion

¼ cup (60g) yellow mustard seeds

¼ teaspoon ground cloves

1 teaspoon ground allspice

1 quart (1 liter) white wine vinegar

½ cup (125g) organic sugar, or to taste

4 garlic cloves, minced, optional

Core and shred the cabbage and toss with 3 tablespoons (45g) salt in a colander set over a large work bowl. Set aside for 1 hour for the cabbage to drain. Rinse the drained cabbage and transfer to a deep work bowl; discard the liquid.

Sterilize the jar(s), lid(s), and ring(s) in a saucepan of lightly boiling water and set aside.

Remove the seeds and veins from the bell and jalapeño peppers and finely chop them. Add to the bowl with the cabbage, then add the onion and mix in the mustard seeds, cloves, and allspice. Transfer the vegetable mixture to the prepared jar(s).

In a large nonreactive preserving pan, combine the vinegar, sugar, and remaining salt. Place over medium-high heat and bring just to a rolling boil, then immediately pour the hot brine over the vegetable mixture. Add the garlic, if using, and seal (see page 17).

This will keep for up to 2 years in a cool, dark place, although it is best when consumed within 9 months.

Korean-Style Sweet and Sour Bamboo Shoots

Do not be tempted to eat raw bamboo shoots: All bamboo contains hydrocyanic acid—a toxin that gives the shoots a bitter taste—which is fully neutralized by blanching. This is a defense mechanism to protect the plant from animals that would otherwise decimate its tender shoots. I particularly like the way kombu (seaweed) changes the flavor profile of this recipe but add it only if you wish. The basic flavor of bamboo shoots is similar to artichokes; kombu shifts this flavor profile in an earthier direction, toward toasted nuts. To add kombu, soften the seaweed in warm water (see page 135 for details) for about thirty to forty-five minutes, then drain and cut into bite-size pieces. Combine with the prepared bamboo shoots, then add the boiling brine as directed. For more information on growing your own bamboo, see page 199.

Yield: 1 quart (1 liter)—I use narrow-mouthed jars to keep the shoots from migrating upward toward the lid

1 to 2 tablespoons (15 to 30g) kosher sea salt, plus more as needed

1 pound (500g) prepared (poached and trimmed) bamboo shoots (weight after trimming)

1 cup (250ml) Green Shiso Vinegar (page 197)

1 cup (250ml) mirin

¼ cup (60g) organic sugar

½ cup (125ml) fish sauce

1 tablespoon (5g) Korean chile flakes (*gochugaru*)

10 strips kombu, softened (see headnote), optional

To yield trimmed, poached shoots ready for pickling: Fill a large work bowl with cold water, add enough salt so the water is as salty as seawater, and set aside. Trim off about 1 inch (2cm) from the base of each bamboo shoot, then cut the shoots in half lengthwise. Strip off the outer leaves and immerse the tender hearts in the cold salt water. Exposure to air will toughen the shoots, so keep them submerged until ready to poach.

Transfer the trimmed shoots to a large nonreactive preserving pan and cover with fresh water. Bring to a gentle boil over medium heat and cook for 10 to 15 minutes (larger varieties will need longer). Remove and rinse under cold running water. Taste a small piece from one of the shoots, and if you can detect bitterness, repeat the previous step, but shorten cooking time to 5 to 8 minutes, depending on size. Once the bitterness has been neutralized, return the poached shoots to fresh salted water until you are ready to pickle.

Sterilize the jar(s), lid(s), and ring(s) in a saucepan of lightly boiling water and set aside. Drain the poached shoots and transfer to the prepared jar(s). Add the chopped kombu, if using.

In a large nonreactive preserving pan, combine the vinegar, mirin, and sugar and bring to a gentle boil over medium-high heat. Immediately remove from the heat and add the fish sauce and chile flakes, then pour the brine over the shoots. Close with a sterilized lid and set aside to cool. Once cooled, transfer to the refrigerator and let rest for 2 weeks before using (no further processing is needed). This will keep for 6 months under refrigeration, but the flavor is best within 2 months.

Mustard Quince

This is a tasty preserve that is excellent with roasts, grilled fish, and poultry. The preserved fruit will turn yellow and resemble sliced peaches. Exact poaching time depends on the ripeness of the fruit: The riper and softer the fruit the shorter the poaching time will be. For best flavor, use quince at the peak of ripeness, when the highly fragrant fruit will perfume the entire kitchen.

Yield: 3½ pints (approximately 1.4 liters)

2 pounds (1kg) ripe quince, peeled and cored (about 4 large)

1 medium onion (8 ounces/250g), cut in half lengthwise, then thinly sliced

2½ cups (625ml) white wine vinegar

1 cup (250ml) honey

1 cup (250g) organic sugar

1½ tablespoons (25g) kosher sea salt

1 tablespoon (10g) yellow mustard seeds

¼ cup (60ml) Dijon mustard

16 juniper berries

8 fresh bay leaves

Sterilize the jar(s), lid(s), and ring(s) in a saucepan of lightly boiling water and set aside.

Shred the quince on the large holes of a vegetable grater, then combine with the sliced onion in a large work bowl, cover, and set aside.

In a deep nonreactive preserving pan, mix the vinegar, honey, sugar, salt, mustard seeds, Dijon mustard, juniper berries, and 4 freshly bruised bay leaves. Set over medium-high heat and bring to a hard, rolling boil. Cook until the liquid is reduced by one quarter, about 8 minutes, then reduce the heat to a gentle simmer. Add the quince mixture, cover, and cook until the shreds of quince are tender, about another 10 minutes. Transfer to the prepared jar(s), place the remaining 4 bay leaves on top of the quince mixture in the jar(s), and seal (see page 17). Store in a cool, dark place for up to 2 years, but the flavor is best when consumed within 9 months.

Old Polish Mustard (*Mustarda Polska*)

I found this recipe in Stanislaus Czerniecki's 1682 *Compendium Ferculorum* ("A Collection of Dishes"), the first cookbook printed in Polish. While he recommended sugar, honey works much better, although no additional sweetener is required. In fact, the only thing it needs is a little vinegar stirred in right before serving. Furthermore, I have added a few ingredients to help enhance the flavor. Using tarragon or garlic vinegar instead of white wine vinegar will change the outcome dramatically, and if you add ground coriander, even more subtle nuances come to the fore. It all depends on what you plan to serve with the mustard.

Yield: 2 cups (500ml)

1 cup (150g) raisins

1½ cups (375ml) light, fruity white wine (such as *vinho verde* or Grüner Veltliner), plus more if needed

1¼ cups (200g) black mustard seeds

9 tablespoons (90g) yellow mustard seeds

1 tablespoon (5g) ground horseradish

2 teaspoons kosher sea salt

2 teaspoons ground caraway

½ cup (125ml) white wine vinegar, plus more if needed

Honey t otaste, for seving, optional

In a small work bowl, cover the raisins with 1 cup (250ml) of the wine. Let sit for at least 8 hours or overnight, until the fruit is soft, then transfer all to a small saucepan. Add the remaining ½ cup (125ml) wine, cover, and bring to a gentle boil over medium heat. Cook until the raisins are plumped and soft, 5 to 6 minutes. While hot, blend in a blender or food processor and set aside.

Grind the black mustard seeds in a spice mill and sift through a fine sieve similar to a tea strainer. Add to the raisin puree.

Preheat the oven to 350°F (175°C).

Spread the yellow mustard seeds on a small baking sheet. Toast, shaking the sheet occasionally, until the seeds achieve a nutty aroma, 5 to 6 minutes (the seeds will smell like popcorn). Remove the toasted seeds from the oven, grind in a spice mill, sift through a fine sieve, and add to the raisin puree along with the horseradish, salt, and caraway. Mix in the vinegar, transfer to a glass jar or a small sterilized crock, cover, and let stand at room temperature for 3 days to allow the flavors to meld and improve. Thin with additional white wine or vinegar (depending on how you want to use the mustard—vinegar will supply a sharper taste).

To can the mustard in small jelly jars, simply sterilize the jar(s), lid(s), and ring(s) in a saucepan of lightly boiling water. Fill the hot jars with the mustard and heat for 5 minutes in the microwave, then seal (see page 17). Overcooking will destroy the flavors. Furthermore, this does not require elaborate processing because the mustard is quite stable at ambient temperatures. It will keep for at least 3 years under refrigeration or simply in a cool, dark closet.

Before serving, taste and adjust the sweetness with honey as desired.

Pickled Brown Figs

The best brown figs to use in this recipe are under-ripe green ones, with patches of brown on the skin; that said, even ripe brown figs are on the dry side and are less likely to turn overly soft in pickle recipes than other varieties. Due to the size and shape of figs, the ideal container for this pickle is a 3-quart (3-liter) square glass jar with a snap-down (clamp-type) lid. I like the Italian brand Fido (see Sources, page 199).

For best flavor, use equal quantities of sage and bay leaves. While the bay adds flavor, it also helps to maintain the firm texture of the figs—but do not substitute dried bay leaves. This is an excellent condiment to serve with roast game, poultry, or veal.

Yield: 3 quarts (3 liters; see headnote)

2½ pounds (1.25kg) under-ripe brown figs with stems attached

½ cup (25g) dried myrtle berries

1 medium red onion (12 ounces/375g), sliced in half lengthwise, then thinly sliced

20 fresh sage leaves

20 fresh bay leaves

10 whole allspice berries

Zest of 1 lemon, shaved in wide strips with a vegetable peeler

2½ cups (625ml) dry red wine

2 cups (500ml) red wine vinegar

¼ cup (60g) kosher sea salt

1 cup (250g) organic sugar

Sterilize a large, square 3-quart (3-liter) canning jar and lid in a pot of lightly boiling water and set aside.

With a clean, sharp paring knife, cut into the blossom end of each fig, so that the blade penetrates the seed mass; do not halve the fruit. In a large work bowl, combine the figs, myrtle, onion, sage, bay leaves, allspice, and lemon zest. Transfer the mixture to the prepared jar.

In a large nonreactive preserving pan, combine 4 cups (1 liter) spring water with the wine, vinegar, salt, and sugar. Set over medium-high heat and bring to a full, rolling boil. Boil for 2 minutes, then pour the hot brine over the fig mixture and clamp or close the lid tightly (no further processing is needed). Once the pickle cools to room temperature, store in a cool place or refrigerate for 2 weeks before using. The pickle will keep in a cool, dark place for up to 6 months.

Pickled Cabbage Relish (Pepper Cabbage)

My grandmother made sure this was always on the table at Thanksgiving and Christmas. I am fairly certain that the recipe comes from one of my grandfather's Lancaster County cousins because I have run across similar dishes throughout the Dutch Country. If there is an overabundance of fall cabbage, here is one way to make good use of it. This wholesome, old-fashioned pickle is very good served cold or room temperature with fried fish, scrapple, fried oysters, chicken salad, and all picnic foods in general.

Yield: 3 quarts (3 liters)—I usually use eight 12-ounce (375-ml) jars

2 cups (250g) finely diced sweet green pepper

2 cups (250g) finely diced sweet red pepper

2 cups (250g) finely chopped onion

8 cups (2kg) finely minced cabbage

2 cups (250g) finely diced celery

¼ cup (60g) kosher sea salt

1 tablespoon (10g) celery seeds

6 tablespoons (60g) yellow mustard seeds

1¼ cups (310g) organic sugar

3 cups (750ml) distilled white vinegar

Ground hot pepper, optional

Sterilize the jar(s), lid(s), and ring(s) in a saucepan of lightly boiling water and set aside.

In a deep nonreactive preserving pan, combine the sweet peppers, onion, cabbage, celery, salt, celery seeds, mustard seeds, sugar, vinegar, and hot pepper, if using. Place over medium heat and bring just to a boil, then reduce the heat and stew until the vegetables are tender, 35 to 45 minutes. Transfer to the prepared jar(s) and seal (see page 17). The relish will keep for up to 2 years stored in a cool, dark place, but is best when consumed within 9 months.

Quince Chutney

Even though they are a close relative of apples and pears, quince stand in a class of their own. Known since ancient times and sacred to Aphrodite, quince is one of the most highly perfumed and seductive of all our orchard fruits. A bowl of freshly picked quince standing in the kitchen will fill the entire house with hints of vanilla, honey, cinnamon, rosewater, and pineapple. Capturing that unique and ephemeral aroma in chutney means cooking the fruit gently, and with the peels left on. Not only does this hold the diced fruit together, but there is huge flavor buried in the skins, and the extra zap of pectin gives this chutney its full-bodied texture.

Yield: 4 pints (2 liters)—I usually use four 1-pint (500-ml) jars

2½ cups (625ml) white wine vinegar

2 cups (500ml) rosé wine

1 tablespoon (15g) kosher sea salt

7 cups (1.75kg) organic sugar

5 pounds (2.5kg) ripe quince, cored and cut into small dice (do not peel)

Grated zest of 1 orange

2 teaspoons powdered star anise

8 fresh bay leaves

Sterilize the jar(s), lid(s), and ring(s) in a saucepan of lightly boiling water and set aside.

In large nonreactive preserving pan, combine the vinegar, wine, salt, and sugar. Set over medium-high heat and bring just to a rolling boil. Reduce the heat to low and add the quince, orange zest, and star anise. Simmer until the fruit is pink, about 25 minutes.

Divide half of the bay leaves among the prepared jars. Transfer the hot quince mixture to the jars, divide the remaining bay leaves on top, and seal (see page 17). This chutney will keep for up to 2 years in a cool, dark place, but is best consumed within 1 year.

Pennsylvania Dutch Pickled Peaches and Tomatoes

Most pickled peach recipes are over-spiced with cloves and cinnamon. The rich flavor of fresh August peaches is easily lost in that approach. Happily, the Pennsylvania Dutch penchant for combining peaches and tomatoes challenges that mind-set because the result is not overly sweet and pairs beautifully with poultry, lamb, and pork. In short, this pickle moves peaches and tomatoes into a middle ground where they can be used as a condiment with meats or with the addition of a little sugar or honey as a filling in dessert pies. I like adding whole small yellow tomatoes as a third, ornamental element to the recipe. The main thing is to strike a balance between the two fruits, so they complement each other. Quartering the fruit will ensure that it remains intact after the hot syrup is added; if sliced too thin, the fruit will fall apart (do not be concerned by fruit shrinkage after a few days in the jar). If you prefer a spicier pickle, add the loose spices directly to the fruit mixture, making sure they are evenly distributed and do not sink to the bottom.

Yield: 2 quarts (2 liters)

1 to 1¼ pounds (500 to 625g) firm Roma-type red paste tomatoes (about 4 large)

3 to 3½ pounds (1.5 to 1.75kg) firm, under-ripe yellow peaches (about 4 large)

Zest of 1 lemon, shaved with a vegetable peeler

10 fresh bay leaves

1½ tablespoons whole allspice berries

2 tablespoons (10g) shredded mace

4 cups (1kg) organic sugar

2 cups (500ml) white wine vinegar

Sterilize a wide-mouthed 2-quart (2-liter) canning jar, lid, and ring in a saucepan of lightly boiling water and set aside.

Bring a large nonreactive preserving pan of water to a rolling boil, then reduce the heat to a quivering simmer. Add the tomatoes and poach for 1 minute, only long enough to heat and loosen the skins. Once a split appears, remove quickly from the pan and rinse under cold water. Gently peel away the skins and cut each tomato into quarters, then set aside.

Pare and pit the peaches, then cut the fruit into quarters. Pack the peeled tomatoes, quartered peaches, strips of lemon zest, and bay leaves into the prepared jar, alternating the fruit to create a red and yellow pattern.

Combine the allspice and mace in a small spice bag or bundle of cheesecloth and tie securely. Rinse the preserving pan and add the sugar, vinegar, and spices. Bring to a boil over medium heat and boil for 8 minutes, then remove the spice bag and pour the syrup over the fruit and seal (see page 17). The pickle will keep for up to 3 years in a cool, dark closet; however, due to the acidity of both fruits, it will begin to discolor in the second year, so I suggest using within 9 months for best color and flavor.

Pickled Chayote (Merliton)

Chayote and mirliton are different names for the same tropical vegetable, which is often likened to squash. As a cucurbit, it is related to both squash and cucumbers and can be treated like either one in cookery. Its flavor is bland like zucchini, which also means it will respond well when used in sweet and sour pickles—the pickle gives it character. In this case, I am treating it like under-ripe squash, so that the firm green texture of the fruit is preserved.

To add a little heat (which works very well with chayote), stir 1 tablespoon (5g) cayenne pepper into the vegetable mixture. If you use the same Italian-style square jar as for the Pickled Brown Figs (see page 147), your ingredients will be less tightly packed. As the cooking step draws water out of the vegetables, there may be an increase in excess brine—reheat and pour it over a large bowl of shredded cabbage for a quick wilted cabbage salad.

Yield: 2 quarts (2 liters)

2 pounds (1kg) chayote (about 4 medium)

1 pound (500g) small seedless pickling cucumbers, ends trimmed

1 cup (125g) thinly sliced celery (use small stalks)

1 medium onion (8 ounces/250g), cut in half lengthwise, then thinly sliced

1 cup (125g) finely diced sweet red pepper

6 large garlic cloves, each cut lengthwise into 3 slices

2 tablespoons (20g) yellow mustard seeds

1 tablespoon (10g) whole black peppercorns

1 tablespoon (5g) whole coriander seeds

6 fresh bay leaves

4 cups (1kg) organic sugar

4 cups (1 liter) distilled white vinegar

¼ cup (60g) kosher sea salt

Sterilize a 2-quart (2-liter), square wide-mouthed jar and lid in a saucepan of lightly boiling water and set aside.

Quarter the chayotes, remove the seeds, then slice the quarters lengthwise into ½-inch-thick (1.25-mm) strips. Place in a deep nonreactive preserving pan. Slice the trimmed cucumbers into ½-inch-thick (1.25-cm) coins and add them to the chayote along with the celery, onion, red pepper, garlic, mustard seeds, black peppercorns, coriander seeds, and bay leaves.

In a large sauce pan, combine the sugar, vinegar, and salt. Place over medium heat, bring to a rolling boil, and boil for 5 minutes, then pour the hot brine over the vegetables. Set the vegetable mixture over medium-high heat and cook just until the vegetables change color, 8 to 10 minutes.

Drain the vegetables, reserving the pickling liquid, and pack the mixture into the prepared jar. Return the reserved pickling liquidto the saucepan, place over medium heat, and bring to a full boil. Boil for 3 minutes, then pour the hot brine over the vegetables and seal the jar (see page 17). If you are using a European-style square jar with a rubber seal and clamp lid, which cannot be microwaved, give it a 15-minute water bath instead.

This will keep for up to 3 years in a cool, dark place, but is best when consumed within 1 year.

Pickled Crab Apples

Many vintage recipes for pickled crab apples called for grape leaves or cherry leaves to help the fruit stay firm and crispy—most classic heirloom crab apple varieties were grown for hard cider, and thus quickly turned to mush when cooked. However, one of the best varieties for pickling is called Callaway, which also makes a beautiful dwarf white-flowering spring ornamental tree. Considered a connoisseur's crab apple, Callaway originated at the Callaway Resort and Gardens in LaGrange, Georgia. The flavor of the fresh-picked fruit is juicy and refreshing, with a hint of spicy wine. The cranberry-red fruit will hold together when cooked, making it ideal for pickling. Whatever variety you choose, leave the fruit whole, unpeeled, and with the stems intact.

Yield: 4 pints (2 liters)

4 cups (1kg) organic sugar

1 quart (1 liter) apple cider vinegar
(or crab apple vinegar, if you can get it)

2 cinnamon sticks

1 tablespoon (15g) whole cassia buds

2 whole star anise pods

1 teaspoon shredded mace

2 pounds (1kg) crab apples, washed thoroughly

2 tablespoons (30ml) honey

In a deep nonreactive preserving pan, combine the sugar and vinegar. Combine the cinnamon sticks, cassia, star anise, and mace in a linen spice bag or double layer of cheesecloth and tie securely. Bruise the spices by gently rolling over the bag once or twice with a rolling pin, then add the bundle to the preserving pan.

Set the preserving pan over medium-high heat, bring to a rolling boil, and boil for 5 minutes. Reduce the heat to a simmer, add the crab apples, and poach just until the skins begin to crack, no more than 5 minutes. Remove from the heat, cover the pan, and let stand overnight.

The next day, sterilize the jar(s), lid(s), and ring(s) in a saucepan of lightly boiling water and set aside. Strain out the fruit and gently pack it into the prepared jars; reserve the poaching liquid but remove and discard the spice bag. Add the honey to the poaching liquid and set over medium-high heat. Cook until the liquid attains the consistency of thin syrup, then pour over the fruit and seal (see page 17). Store in a cool, dark for up to 3 years, but the pickle's flavor and texture are best when consumed within 9 months.

Pickled Garlic Scapes

For the uninitiated, garlic scapes are the delicate and underutilized flower heads of common garlic. Garlic is planted in the fall after the first frost so that it can vernalize over the winter. Unlike many plants, it grows quietly under the snow and needs that winterizing experience to produce well-developed bulbs the following season; this is because the genetic origin of garlic is high-altitude central Asia. When garlics bloom the following spring, they invest all their energy in growing scapes—which is why garlic scapes need to be removed, to reroute that all-important energy to the cloves. For best texture, harvest the scapes as they begin to uncurl; once erect they will be tough and stringy. Trim them by snipping off the tips of the flower heads and the tough base of each stem.

If including the jalapeño, add it with or in place of the red bell pepper. The choice of herbs is entirely personal but will further define the pickle's flavor. For many years, I used fresh dill before discovering that thyme takes the pickle in another direction altogether, and lemon thyme is more special, still; lacking that herb, add tiny shreds of lemon zest. Add allspice if you like—the sky is the limit—but only after first perfecting the recipe below, then decide how you want to personalize it to your own tastes. Serve as a side dish drizzled liberally with fresh lemon juice.

Yield: 2 quarts (2 liters)

1 pound (500g) trimmed garlic scapes
(weight after trimming; see headnote)

10 fresh bay leaves

1 medium onion (8 ounces/250g), cut in half lengthwise, then thinly sliced

1 large red bell pepper, cut into narrow strips

4 jalapeño peppers (4 ounces/125g), seeded and cut into strips, optional (see headnote)

6 garlic cloves, cut lengthwise into thin slices

1 tablespoon (5g) whole coriander seeds

1 tablespoon (10g) white mustard seeds

1 teaspoon whole black peppercorns

1 large bunch fresh herbs, such as fresh dill (preferably blossom heads with small green seeds), lemon thyme, or thyme, or to taste (see headnote)

3 cups (750ml) white wine vinegar

¼ cup (60g) kosher sea salt

¾ cup (185) organic sugar

Sterilize a 3½- to 4-quart (3.5- to 4-liter) jar, lid, and ring in a large pot of lightly boiling water and set aside.

Bring a large nonreactive preserving pan of water to boil over medium-high heat. Reduce the heat and poach the garlic scapes gently until tender but not soft, about 5 minutes (precise poaching time varies depending on variety of garlic scape used). Drain (see note) and transfer the garlic scapes to the prepared jar. Add the bay leaves, onion, red pepper, jalapeño, if using, the garlic, coriander seeds, mustard seeds, peppercorns, and fresh herbs.

Rinse the preserving pan and combine the vinegar, salt, and sugar with 5 cups (1.25 liters) spring water in the pan. Set over medium heat and bring to a rolling boil, then pour the hot brine over the garlic scape mixture. Stir with a wooden spoon, then cover the jar tightly. Let stand until cooled, then transfer to the refrigerator or store in a cool, dark place away from direct sunlight (no further processing is needed). After 2 weeks, the pickle is ready to serve. This unique pickle will keep for as long as 3 years when stored in a cool, dark place, but is best consumed within 2 years.

Note: Recycle the poaching broth as a flavorful vegetarian base for soup stock. Poach the garlic scape trimmings in this same broth to double the flavor, then strain and reserve or freeze for later use.

Pickled Jerusalem Artichokes

In this heirloom sweet-and-sour recipe, the Jerusalem artichokes remain crunchy while the pleasant, mellow brine counterbalances the somewhat earthy flavor of the vegetables. Do not hold back on the thyme—it enhances the flavor.

Yield: 2 quarts (2 liters)

2 pounds (1kg) scrubbed and trimmed Jerusalem artichokes (weight after trimming), cut into irregular bite-size pieces

12 fresh bay leaves

1 medium onion (8 ounces/250g), cut in half lengthwise, then thinly sliced

6 garlic cloves, cut in half lengthwise

1 tablespoon (5g) fresh thyme leaves or several sprigs of thyme, to taste

1 tablespoon (10g) whole black peppercorns

6 whole cloves

3¼ cups (815ml) white wine vinegar

1 cup (250g) organic sugar

2 tablespoons (30g) kosher sea salt

Sterilize the jar(s), lid(s), and ring(s) in a saucepan of lightly boiling water and set aside.

In a deep work bowl, mix the prepared Jerusalem artichokes, the bay leaves, onion, garlic, thyme, peppercorns, and cloves until combined, then transfer to the prepared jar(s). Set aside in a pan of hot water to keep hot while you prepare the brine.

In a deep nonreactive preserving pan, combine the vinegar, sugar, and salt with 1½ cups (375ml) spring water. Place over medium-high heat and bring just to a rolling boil, then immediately pour the hot brine over the vegetables and seal (see page 17). Let stand in a cool place away from direct sunlight for 1 to 2 weeks to mature before using. Stored in a cool, dark place, the pickle will keep for up to 6 months; in the refrigerator, it will keep for about 1 year before the artichokes begin to soften.

Louisiana-Style Pickled Pumpkin with Chayote (Merliton)

This beautiful pickle is best when several different kinds of pumpkin are used—yellow-, white-, and orange-fleshed types all work. You can even use summer squash like yellow crookneck; just be certain that your fruit is firm. Furthermore, if you can find a mix of tiny okras of different colors, this will add to the visual impact: I prefer the heirloom varieties called Red Velvet, Green Velvet, and White Velvet. Do note that you will need to pare off the skin of the pumpkins but not the chayote.

Yield: About 2 quarts (2 liters)

3½ pounds (1.75kg) mixed pumpkin, peeled and cut into 1-inch (2.5-cm) cubes

8 ounces (250g) diced chayote

8 ounces (250g) pared and sliced mixed yellow, orange, and white carrots (weight after paring and slicing; about 4 medium)

8 ounces (250g) baby okra, tips and stems removed

4 small orange sweet peppers (4 ounces/125g), seeds removed, sliced into rings

¼ cup (25g) hot red pepper, sliced into rings, or to taste (weight after slicing)

1 medium onion (8 ounces/250g), sliced in half lengthwise, then thinly sliced

10 fresh bay leaves

5 cups (2.25 liters) distilled white vinegar

1 cup (250g) organic sugar

2 tablespoons (30g) kosher sea salt

2 tablespoons (50g) whole allspice berries

1 teaspoon whole cloves

1 cup (45g) finely chopped fresh dill

In a deep nonreactive preserving pan, combine the pumpkin, chayote, carrots, okra, sweet peppers, hot pepper, onion, and bay leaves and set aside.

In a large sauce pan pan, combine the vinegar, sugar, salt, allspice, and cloves with 3 cups (750ml) spring water. Place over medium heat, bring the mixture to a boil, and keep at a steady boil for 5 minutes. Pour the hot brine over the pumpkin mixture, cover, and let stand at room temperature overnight.

The next day, bring the mixture to a gentle boil over medium heat and cook until the vegetables are tender but not soft, 25 to 30 minutes, depending on the type of pumpkins used.

While the mixture cooks, sterilize the jar(s), lid(s), and ring(s) in a saucepan of lightly boiling water.

Stir the dill into the pumpkin mixture, then transfer to the prepared jars and seal (see page 17). Store in a cool, dark place to mature for 2 weeks, then serve as needed. It will keep unopened for at least 1 year.

Pickled Purslane with String Beans or Limas

Anyone who gardens is familiar with purslane (*Portulaca oleracea*). It grows wild in most parts of the world and is known by hundreds of colloquial names. While treated as a common weed, the plant was once an important potherb imbued with well-known curative properties as noted in John Evelyn's *Acetaria,* a charming and highly readable 1699 discourse on salads. Purslane stems should be harvested while young, tender, and slightly pink in color, before the plant begins to flower; after flowering, the stems become stringy and flavorless. Strip the stems of their leaves and proceed as instructed. The method of serving was to drain the brine off and drizzle the purslane with olive oil and fresh lemon juice just before sending it to the table. Leftover pickle juice can be recycled into salad dressings.

I have introduced beans into this recipe because they add a nice flavor contrast to the purslane, plus eye appeal. Any sort of common string bean will work here; as for limas, there are several heirloom varieties with colorful patterns. Two I recommend are Sadie's baby lima (a Pennsylvania Dutch heirloom—see Sadie Kriebel's Dill Tomatoes, page 106), and Jackson Wonder bush lima, an 1888 heirloom from Georgia. If you like, you can use a combination of string beans and limas.

Yield: 1 pint (500ml)—this recipe scales up easily

4 ounces (125g) purslane stems, stripped of their leaves and cut into 2-inch (5-cm) lengths

½ lemon

½ cup (2 ounces/60g) fresh baby lima beans, plus ½ cup (2 ounces/60g) fresh ornamental

lima beans or 1 cup (4 ounces/125g) string beans cut into segments and sliced

4 small fresh bay leaves

6 whole allspice berries

Two 2-inch-long (5-cm) slices fresh ginger

⅓ cup (90ml) dry white wine

⅓ cup (90ml) white wine vinegar

2 tablespoons (30g) organic sugar

2 teaspoons kosher sea salt

Sterilize the jar(s), lid(s), and ring(s) in a saucepan of lightly boiling water and set aside.

In a small nonreactive preserving pan, bring 1-quart 1 liter) spring water to a rolling boil over medium-high heat. Juice the lemon half into the water and add the lemon as well. Reduce the heat to a gentle simmer, add the purslane stems, and poach for exactly 1½ minutes, until hot, then immediately remove them from the hot water and run under cold water. Drain well and combine with the beans, bay leaves, allspice, and ginger in a work bowl. Transfer the vegetable mixture to the prepared jar(s).

Rinse the preserving pan and combine the white wine, vinegar, sugar, and salt in the pan with ⅓ cup (90ml) spring water. Bring to a rolling boil over medium-high heat, pour the hot brine over the vegetable mixture, and seal (see page 17). Allow the pickle to mellow for 2 weeks before serving. This will keep for at least 2 years when stored in a cool, dark closet, but I recommend consuming it within 9 months otherwise the delicate flavors begin to fade.

Pickled Radish Pods

To be honest, you should already like radishes before exploring the young seed pods as food. While the tender green pods are mild in comparison to the crunchy roots, they are radishes nonetheless, with the same heat and sinus-clearing properties. So, if your view of radishes is dim, they might redeem themselves as a homey cold remedy and even better as a zippy appetizer. Any young pods will work for this application—especially those of the Madras podding radish (developed in India exclusively for pickling; see Sources, page 199), but select only the youngest, greenest, and most tender pods when harvesting; older pods may be stringy or filled with pith.

Incidentally, I enjoy adding small vegetable curiosities to this pickle, among them the tightly coiled pods of a legume known as Snails (*Medicago scutellata*). Kids love them, and the young green pods can also be added raw to salads.

Yield: 2 pints (1 liter)

2 garlic cloves, cut in half lengthwise

6 whole cloves

1 teaspoon white mustard seeds

1 teaspoon whole black peppercorns

6 fresh bay leaves

1 small onion (less than 8 ounces/250g), cut in half lengthwise, then thinly sliced

Four 2-inch (5-cm) slices fresh horseradish

8 ounces (250g) radish pods

1½ cups (375ml) white wine vinegar

¾ cup (180ml) dry white wine

2 tablespoons (30g) kosher sea salt

½ cup (125g) organic sugar

Sterilize two 1-pint (500-ml) jars, lids, and rings in a saucepan of lightly boiling water. Divide the garlic, cloves, mustard seeds, peppercorns, bay leaves, onion, and horseradish between the prepared jars. Add the radish pods and mix evenly.

In a nonreactive medium preserving pan, combine the vinegar, wine, salt, and sugar with 1 cup (250ml) spring water and set over medium heat. Bring to a rolling boil and boil for 3 minutes, then pour the hot brine over the vegetable mixture and seal (see page 17). Stored in a cool, dark place, the pickle will keep for at least 1 year.

Pickled Rock Samphire

Rock samphire (*Crithmum maritimum*) is salty when eaten raw, but not unpleasantly so, and its subtler flavors become much more pronounced when it is infused in cold water for one to two hours before cooking.

While in northern France several years ago, I managed to find a few jars of Restaurant Perard's delicious *rameaux salpicon*, and after tasting it, came up with this close approximation. Of course, there is no substitute for going to Le Touquet and enjoying the old French ladies who congregate in the restaurant with their knitting, not to mention the homey fish cookery of chez Perard, but this recipe will at least transport the palate and the imagination to that unusual place until you get your passport renewed. Regarding the carrots, these are included purely for ornamental purposes, so the exact nature and number of slices is up to you; however, too many tend to clutter the pickle. Fancy shapes, such as flowers, stars, triangles, or whatever suits your fancy, can be made with small vegetable cutters or a sharp paring knife.

Yield: 2½ pints (1.25 liters)

1 pound (500g) fresh samphire, trimmed of roots

3 garlic cloves, cut in half lengthwise

8 slices carrot, cut into fancy shapes (see headnote)

15 whole cloves

1 teaspoon yellow mustard seeds

1 teaspoon mixed whole peppercorns (white, red, green, and black)

6 fresh bay leaves

1 small onion (less than 8 ounces/250g), sliced paper thin

3 cups (750m) white wine vinegar

1½ cups (375m) dry white wine

¼ cup (60g) kosher sea salt

¼ cup (60g) organic sugar

Trim off and discard any stems from the samphire that are tough or turning black. In a deep work bowl, cover the samphire with cold water. Let sit uncovered for 1 to 2 hours at room temperature to draw off the saltiness. Drain and pat dry with paper towels or dry in a salad spinner. Return to the work bowl and mix in the garlic, carrot, cloves, mustard seeds, peppercorns, bay leaves, and onion until combined and the ingredients are well distributed.

Sterilize a 1½-quart (1.5 liter) wide-mouthed canning jar, lid, and ring in a saucepan of lightly boiling water. Pack the samphire mixture into the prepared jar.

In a large nonreactive preserving pan, combine the vinegar, wine, salt, and sugar with 2 cups (500ml) spring water. Place over medium heat and bring to a rolling boil. Boil for 5 minutes, then pour the hot brine into the jar, pressing down so the samphire mixture remains submerged, and seal (see page 17). Refrigerate for at least 1 month before using.

The flavor improves over time, but do not keep this for longer than 2 years.

Pickled West Indian Burr Gherkins

Although they originated in Africa, burr gherkins (*Cucumis anguria*) were first introduced to the United States from Jamaica in 1793. They are considered an heirloom in the African-American culinary tradition and are one of the easiest, most prolific, and most pest-free plants to grow in the garden. It is the tiny fruits—before they develop seeds—that are preferred for pickles. In early American kitchens, this relative of the cucumber took the place of true French cornichons and as such were a favorite condiment with oysters and shellfish. For this reason, I highly recommend using the fish pepper as the hot pepper for this recipe; however, any spicy red pepper will do.

Yield: 1 quart (1 liter)

1¼ pounds (625g) tiny burr gherkins, trimmed of stems

10 white pearl onions, peeled and cut in half lengthwise

4 garlic cloves, cut in half lengthwise

4 fresh bay leaves

1 tablespoon (15g) minced hot red pepper, or to taste

1 teaspoon whole allspice berries

1 teaspoon yellow mustard seeds

1½ cups (325ml) white wine vinegar

6 tablespoons (90g) organic sugar

2 tablespoons (30g) kosher sea salt

Sterilize a 1-quart (1-liter) wide-mouthed canning jar, lid, and ring in a saucepan of lightly boiling water.

In a deep work bowl, combine the burr gherkins, pearl onions, garlic, bay leaves, hot red pepper, allspice, and mustard seeds. Pack the mixture into the prepared jar as tightly as possible.

In a small nonreactive preserving pan, combine the vinegar, sugar, and salt with ⅔ cup (160ml) spring water. Set over medium-high heat, bring to a full rolling boil, and boil for 3 minutes. Pour the hot brine over the vegetable mixture and seal (see page 17). This will keep for at least 2 years when stored in a cool, dark place, but I recommend consuming it within 1 year.

Pottsville Pickle

This pickle takes its name from an early circa-1900s cookbook published in Pottsville, Pennsylvania. It became one of the most popular chow-chow-type recipes in the region. Friends in Maine have even taken blue ribbons for it at their state fair! I think it is best served with smoked sausages and beer, and if what grows together truly goes together, the beer of choice will be Yuengling—brewed in Pottsville since 1829.

Yield: 6 pints (3 liters)

3 cups (500g) diced ripe red tomato

3 cups (450g) diced green (unripe) tomato

3 cups (375g) finely shredded cabbage

3 cups (500g) chopped onion

3 cups (375g) chopped celery (stems only; no leaves)

1½ cups (225g) finely chopped red bell pepper

¼ cup (60g) kosher sea salt

½ cup (50g) finely grated fresh horseradish

¼ cup (40g) yellow mustard seeds

3 cups (750g) organic sugar

3 cups (750ml) distilled white vinegar

½ teaspoon ground cloves

½ teaspoon ground cinnamon

In a large nonreactive work bowl; preferably glass or stoneware, combine the red and green tomatoes, the cabbage, onion, celery, and bell pepper. Toss gently with the salt and let the vegetables drain uncovered at room temperature overnight. The next day, press out and discard excess liquid, but do not rinse the vegetables. Add the horseradish and mustard seeds and transfer the mixture to a large nonreactive preserving pan.

In a large saucepan, combine the sugar and vinegar. Place over medium heat and bring to a hard, rolling boil. Immediately pour the hot brine over the vegetable mixture and set over medium heat. Cook for exactly 25 minutes, just enough to tenderize the vegetables, then add the cloves and cinnamon. While the mixture cooks, sterilize the jar(s), lid(s), and ring(s) in a saucepan of lightly boiling water and set aside.

Transfer to the prepared jar(s) and seal (see page 17); if you prefer the water bath method, allow 15 minutes. This pickle will keep for at least 3 years in a cool, dark place, but is best consumed within 1 year.

Japanese-Style Seaweed Pickle

The dried seaweed varieties necessary for this pickle may be found in Japanese or Korean markets. Kombu is relatively common and widely used because it contains glutamate, a flavor enhancer. *Me hijiki* is sold loose and resembles shredded black tea leaves; it gives the recipe its bulk. *Fujisawa aosako* is sold loose as well but resembles dried parsley, adding flecks of color and an unusual chive-like flavor. To serve, drain the brine and season the pickle with a dash of *shichimi togarashi* (a Japanese seven-spice blend) or drizzle liberally with toasted sesame oil and scatter sesame seeds over the top.

Yield: 2 quarts (2 liters)

3 ounces (90g) dried kombu

3½ ounces (100g) dried *me hijiki*

2 tablespoons (10g) powdered bonito dashi (about 4 packets)

¼ cup (20g) dried *fujisawa aosako*

¼ cup (30g) diced hot red peppers (or slice them into tiny rings)

¾ cup (125g) light brown sugar

2 cups (500ml) Green Shiso Vinegar (page 197)

¼ cup (60ml) light soy sauce (*usukuchi shoyu*)

¼ cup (60ml) Shaoxing cooking wine or dry sherry

1 tablespoon (15g) kosher sea salt

Put the kombu and *me hijiki* in separate work bowls and cover with boiling water; cover the *me hijiki* with a towel so that it swells in its own steam. Let sit for 30 minutes to tenderize. While the seaweed is soaking, dissolve the dashi powder in 2 cups (500ml) spring water in a nonreactive preserving pan and set aside.

Sterilize a 2-quart (2-liter) canning jar, lid, and ring in a saucepan of lightly boiling water and set aside.

Once tender, drain the *me hijiki* in a sieve and gently press out any excess liquid (save it for soup stock), then transfer to a clean work bowl. Add the dried *fujisawa aosako* and hot peppers. Drain the kombu and, with a sharp knife, slice it into a combination of narrow, pasta-like shreds and small squares. Stir the kombu into the *me hijiki* mixture, then transfer to the prepared jar.

Set the dashi over medium-high heat and bring just to a rolling boil. Add the sugar, vinegar, soy sauce, wine, and salt. Boil for 3 minutes, then pour the hot brine over the seaweed mixture and seal (see page 17). This pickle will keep in a cool, dark place for at least 2 years. Though some believe that it improves with age, the older the better, this is an acquired taste and I recommend consuming it within 2 years.

Scrapple Sauce

My grandmother obtained this recipe from Margaret Hoopes, a friend of her mother. The original recipe came from Percy Hoopes, a scrapple maker in Chester County, Pennsylvania. Hoopes used to sell his sauce in old-fashioned pickle jars. The secret ingredient in the sauce is sage because scrapple also has sage in it (or should). This sauce is also excellent on smoked pork chops or grilled sausages.

Yield: 6 pints (1.5 liters)

4 quarts (6 pounds/3kg) green (unripe) tomatoes, chopped to a coarse puree

2 cups (300g) very finely chopped onion (to almost a coarse puree)

¼ cup (60g) kosher sea salt

2 cups (500g) organic sugar

3 tablespoons (30g) finely chopped hot pepper, or to taste

3 cups (750ml) apple cider vinegar

1 tablespoon (10g) yellow mustard seeds

2 teaspoons celery seeds

2 tablespoons (50g) freshly grated ginger

⅓ cup (25g) finely minced fresh sage leaves or 2 tablespoons (10g) ground dried sage

1 cup (125g) finely diced sweet red pepper

Sterilize the jar(s), lid(s), and ring(s) in a saucepan of lightly boiling water and set aside.

In a deep preserving pan, combine the tomatoes, onion, salt, sugar, hot peppers, vinegar, mustard seeds, and celery seeds. Set over medium-high heat and cook steadily until the sauce is thick and the liquid is reduced by one-quarter, about 30 minutes. Add the ginger, sage, and sweet red pepper and continue cooking for 10 to 15 minutes, until the red pepper is tender, then transfer the sauce to the prepared jars and seal (see page 17). This sauce will keep for more than 1 year if stored in a cool, dark closet.

Spiced Red Cabbage

This old Pennsylvania farmhouse recipe has been popular since the eighteenth century and there are innumerable variations. I prefer this version because the hot pepper gives the pickle a pleasant kick. You can always cut back on the pepper—or add more. For more complex flavor, add 2 tablespoons (10g) whole coriander seeds and/or 10 garlic cloves sliced in half lengthwise.

Yield: 4 quarts (4 liters)

3½ pounds (1.75kg) red cabbage (about 1½ heads)

½ cup (125g) kosher sea salt

1 large red onion (about 1 pound/500g),
sliced in half lengthwise, then thinly sliced

2 teaspoons celery seeds

1 tablespoon (5g) ground cayenne pepper, or to taste

5 cups (1.25 liters) red wine vinegar

2 cups (500g) organic sugar

1 tablespoon (5g) shredded mace

1 tablespoon (25g) whole allspice berries

3 cinnamon sticks

Finely shred the cabbage and toss it with the salt in a deep work bowl. Transfer to a colander set over a large bowl and let drain at room temperature for 24 hours. Press out the moisture, but do not rinse the cabbage; discard the liquid.

In a deep work bowl, combine the drained cabbage, red onion, celery seeds, and cayenne pepper, then pack the mixture into a 1-gallon (4-liter) earthenware crock or large wide-mouthed glass jar.

In a large nonreactive preserving pan, combine the vinegar and sugar with 1 cup (250ml) spring water. Gather the mace, allspice, and cinnamon sticks in a spice bag or double layer of cheesecloth and tie securely. Add the spices to the vinegar, set over medium-high heat, and bring to a boil. Boil for 8 minutes, then remove the spice bag and pour the hot brine over the cabbage. If using a jar, simply screw on a canning ring and lid; if using a ceramic crock, tie down with cheesecloth and cover with a snug-fitting lid (many come with lids). Store for up to 5 or 6 months in a cool, dark closet or pantry.

If you prefer to put up the spiced cabbage, transfer the cabbage mixture to microwave-safe jars before making the brine. Pour the hot brine over the mixture and seal (see page 17).

Sweet and Sour Grapes with Desert Tarragon

I have always been an admirer of Catherine Emig Plagemann (1905–76), one of our most accomplished Pennsylvania Dutch pickle cooks. No less than M.F.K. Fisher sang her laurels, bringing out a new edition of Plagemann's classic *Fine Preserving* in 1986. This beautiful pink-tinted pickle is inspired by one of Plagemann's, although with a few new twists. Since grapes shrink when pickled, there will be leftover syrup after they are eaten—this syrup is excellent for stewing plums or as a marinade for duck.

Mexican tarragon (*Tagetes lucida*) is a wild cousin of the common marigold, native to the Southwest and Mexico. It is employed extensively in Mexican cooking because its flavor is mellower than French tarragon. While it can be dried for use during the winter, only fresh plants should be used for pickling. In fact, the tiny yellow flowers make a perfect garnish for serving.

Yield: 1 quart (1 liter)

1 pound (500g) stemmed seedless green grapes (weight after stemming and washing)

1 pound (500g) stemmed seedless red grapes (weight after stemming and washing)

2 large shallots (about 4 ounces/125g), very thinly sliced, rings separated

¼ cup (60g) goji berries

1 cup (15g) Mexican tarragon, leaves only, plus several flower heads (see headnote)

8 fresh bay leaves

3 cups (750g) organic sugar

2 tablespoons (30g) preserving salt

2 cups (500ml) white wine vinegar

Sterilize a narrow-mouthed 1-quart (1-liter) canning jar, lid, and ring in a saucepan of lightly boiling water and set aside.

Cut the grapes in half lengthwise, then combine them with the shallots, goji berries, Mexican tarragon, and bay leaves in a large work bowl. Transfer to the prepared jar.

In a medium nonreactive preserving pan, dissolve the sugar and salt in the vinegar. Set over medium-high heat and bring to a rolling boil. Boil for 3 minutes, then pour the hot brine over the grapes and seal (see page 17). Let the pickle mature for at least 1 week before serving. Store in a cool place out of direct light. It is best when used within 6 months.

Sweet and Sour Plums

This is an heirloom Pennsylvania Dutch recipe that appeared in cookbooks as early as 1802, so it is probably much older. As a condiment, it is generally served as a side dish with rich meat dishes, in particular roasts. The secret to its unique flavor and texture lies in the slow, several-day process of drawing out excess water from the fruit. The flavors become concentrated while the liquid gradually develops into a thick syrup. I have tried several shortcuts and none of them produce the same classic results.

Yield: About 5 pints (2.5 liters)

4½ pounds (2.25kg) ripe plums

2⅓ cups (590ml) red wine vinegar

4 cups (1kg) organic sugar

2 teaspoons whole cloves

Two or three 3-inch (7.5-cm) cinnamon sticks, broken into small pieces

Wash the plums, then stick each 5 or 6 times with a skewer or large needle (this allows the brine to penetrate the fruit for pickling). Transfer the plums to a crock or deep work bowl.

In a medium nonreactive preserving pan, combine the vinegar, sugar, cloves, and cinnamon stick pieces. Set over medium-high heat, bring to a boil, and boil for 4 minutes, then pour the hot brine over the plums and let stand overnight.

The next day, strain off the liquid into a saucepan. Set over medium heat and bring just to a boil, then pour over the plums. Let stand overnight again.

On the third day, sterilize the jar(s), lid(s), and ring(s) in a saucepan of lightly boiling water and set aside. Repeat the straining and boiling process with the plums one more time. Once the brine has been poured back over the plums, pack the hot fruit into the prepared jars, distributing the spices evenly. Transfer the syrup to the same saucepan and return to medium-high heat. Bring to a rolling boil and boil for 4 minutes, then pour over the fruit in the jars and seal (see page 17); if you prefer the water bath method, allow 10 minutes.

Stored in a cool, dark place, this pickle will keep for at least 2 years; however, I recommend consuming it within the first 1 year.

Sweet and Sour Green Tomato Pickle

I found this recipe in an old handwritten cookbook, and scribbled beside it was one word, "Good!" So, I decided to try it, and yes indeed, the recipe lives up to expectations. In fact, this is one of the most popular pickles among my circle of friends. I cannot seem to make enough of it! So right before the first frost, do yourself a favor and gather in as many green tomatoes as you can. That effort will repay you with this recipe.

Yield: 5 pints (2.5 liters)

3 pounds (1.5kg) green (unripe) tomatoes, sliced (use small tomatoes)

1 pound (500g) thinly sliced onions

1½ pounds (750g) large bell peppers, sliced (about 6—use a mix of red and green)

2 tablespoons (30g) kosher sea salt, divided

½ teaspoon ground mace

½ teaspoon ground cinnamon

½ teaspoon ground cloves

½ teaspoon ground allspice

4 cups (1kg) organic sugar

1 quart (1 liter) distilled white vinegar

In a deep work bowl, combine the sliced tomatoes, onions, and peppers. Toss gently with 1½ tablespoons (23g) of the salt, then spread out in a colander set over a bowl. Let stand at room temperature uncovered overnight to drain.

The next day, discard the liquid and rinse the vegetables. Transfer to a large bowl filled with ice water and let stand for 1 hour. Drain well, then transfer to a large nonreactive preserving pan and add the mace, cinnamon, cloves, allspice, and the remaining ½ tablespoon (7g) salt.

Sterilize the jar(s), lid(s), and ring(s) in a saucepan of lightly boiling water and set aside.

In a large saucepan, dissolve the sugar in the vinegar and set over medium-high heat. Bring just to a hard boil, then pour the hot brine over the vegetable mixture. Set the mixture over medium heat and cook gently but steadily until tender, about 20 minutes. Transfer the pickle to the prepared jar(s) and seal (see page 17); if you prefer the water bath method, allow 12 minutes. This will keep for at least 3 years in a cool, dark place, although I recommend consuming it within 9 months.

Sweet and Sour Saffron Cauliflower

I owe the inspiration for this cheerfully colored pickle to Philadelphia chef Steven Eckerd, who is one of the most talented Pennsylvania Dutch chefs making waves in the food scene. He and I collaborated to create a *Neideitsch* ("New Wave Dutch") dinner at Drexel University in 2014 as a way of showcasing the culinary potential of our traditional regional cuisine. Chef Eckerd's original dish was served as a salad, which I have transformed here into a mild pickle that can be served as an appetizer or side dish, garnished with chopped chives or finely diced red peppers (or both). It makes a great snack with fried oysters and beer.

Tenderness is the secret to this recipe. It is possible in my part of Pennsylvania to find super-succulent just-picked cauliflowers at farm stands in early fall. If your cauliflower is several days old or came shipped from somewhere else and of unknown age, poach it in boiling water for 2 minutes before combining with the onions and other ingredients. This will ensure its tenderness once in the pickle.

Yield: 2 quarts (2 liters)

1½ pounds (750g) freshly picked cauliflower (see headnote)

2 medium onions (about 1 pound/500g), cut in half lengthwise, then thinly sliced

4 garlic cloves, coarsely chopped

1 tablespoon (5g) whole coriander seeds

1 teaspoon whole dill seeds

1 cup (250ml) white wine vinegar

2 tablespoons (30g) kosher sea salt

½ cup (125g) organic sugar

½ teaspoon ground saffron (ground to a powder in a mortar)

Sterilize a wide-mouthed 2-quart (2-liter) canning jar, lid, and ring in a saucepan of lightly boiling water.

Core the cauliflower and divide it into florets, then cut into bite-size pieces and transfer to a large work bowl. Add the onions, garlic, coriander seeds, and dill seeds and mix thoroughly. Transfer the mixture to the prepared jar.

In a large nonreactive preserving pan, combine the vinegar, salt, sugar, and saffron with 3 cups (750ml) spring water. Set over medium-high heat, bring to a rolling boil, and boil for about 3 minutes, then pour the hot brine over the vegetables and seal (see page 17).

Store in a cool, dark pantry, where it will keep unopened for up to 2 years. Once opened, store it in the refrigerator and use within 6 months.

Sweet and Sour String Beans

I can't remember a meal when this pickle wasn't on my grandmother's table; as invariable as salt and pepper, breakfast or dinner, it was always there. My grandfather could never get enough of these beans, and since the original recipe came from relatives in Lancaster County, it was his way of celebrating his Pennsylvania Dutch roots—not to mention that my grandmother got the recipe down pat.

It was also a way to showcase the beautiful bush beans from the kitchen garden, and I remember well the heaps of freshly harvested Pencil Pod black wax beans (the seeds, not the pods, are black), their bright yellow color standing in rich contrast to the green Landreth Stringless bush beans. The basic idea in this recipe is to mix two colors of beans and stand them on end in the jars so that they create a carnival effect that goes straight to the table once opened.

Therefore, the best string beans for this pickle are the ones with the straightest and most pencil-like round pods. On that point I can also recommend the classic French heirloom bean called Beurre de Rocquencourt for the yellow, and our own Roughwood creation, forty-day Hebron's Tenderette (see Sources, page 199), which you can even grow in tubs if so inclined. If you like a little heat, add up to 3 tablespoons (30g) finely diced hot red pepper.

Yield: 1½ quarts (1.5 liters)

2 pounds (1kg) string beans, trimmed and sliced into 1-inch (2.5-cm) lengths, or your choice of bean

½ large onion (less than 8 ounces/250g), cut in half lengthwise, then thinly sliced

4 ounces (125g) whole pearl onions (about 15, depending on size), peeled

6 garlic cloves, very thinly sliced lengthwise

10 fresh bay leaves

1 teaspoon celery seeds

1 tablespoon (10g) yellow mustard seeds

3 tablespoons (30g) finely diced hot pepper, or to taste, optional

3 cups (750g) organic sugar

3 cups (750ml) white wine vinegar

2 tablespoons (30g) kosher sea salt

Sterilize the jar(s), lid(s), and ring(s) in a saucepan of lightly boiling water and set aside.

Bring a large saucepan of water to a gentle boil over medium-high heat. Add the string beans and poach just until the colors turn bright and the beans are slightly tender, about 4 minutes. Drain and transfer to a large work bowl. Add the onion, pearl onions, cloves, bay leaves, celery seeds, and mustard seeds (if also using hot pepper, add now).

Transfer the mixture to the prepared jar(s) and set aside. In a large nonreactive preserving pan, combine the sugar, vinegar, and salt. Set over medium-high heat, bring to a rolling boil, and boil for 2 minutes, then pour the hot brine over the vegetables and seal (see page 17). Let stand for 3 weeks before serving. The beans will keep for up to 2 years when stored in a cool, dark place, but I suggest consuming them within 1 year.

Vinegar Cherries

This old-fashioned farmhouse recipe from the Pennsylvania Dutch Country is both easy to make and highly adaptable—no cooking required! Any excess juice strained off after three days of infusing can be used to pickle hard-boiled eggs or as a marinade for beets, pork, duck, or game. The pickled cherries are delightful on roast pork or added to a game casserole. Every time I make this, I experiment with new ways to try the pickle.

Yield: 3 pints (1.5 liters)—I usually use three 1-pint (500-ml) jars

3 pounds (1.5kg) pitted sour cherries (weight after pitting)

1 quart (1 liter) apple cider vinegar

4 cups (1kg) organic sugar

One 3-inch (7.5-cm) cinnamon stick

Pit the cherries over a work bowl to collect the juice. Combine the cherries, any juice, and the vinegar in a large nonreactive container (such as a stoneware crock), cover, and let stand to infuse for 3 days. After 3 days, drain the cherries and reserve the brine for salad dressing, mincemeat pies, or marinades.

Measure the cherries—you should have about 6 cups of cherries or 2 pounds (1kg) by weight (the cherries will lose a little water weight while marinating)—and transfer them to a clean nonreactive container. To each 1 cup (165g) cherries, add 1 cup (250g) sugar. Cover and let the cherry and sugar mixture stand for 3 days, stirring from time to time, until the sugar is fully dissolved.

Sterilize the jar(s), lid(s), and ring(s) in a saucepan of lightly boiling water. Strain the cherries from their liquid, then pack them into the prepared jars. Break the cinnamon stick into pieces and divide it evenly among the jars. Close the jars with clean lids and store in a cool place until needed—because of the high acidity, no cooking or further processing is required. The cherries will keep for more than a year stored in a cool place; under refrigeration, they will keep for at least 2 years.

Venetian Pumpkin Mustard (*Mostarda di Zucca Veneziana*)

Traditional Venetian pumpkin preserve is quite famous in northern Italian cookery. The favored local pumpkin for making it is the *zucca marina di Chioggia*, also known as the Chioggia sea pumpkin—if the pumpkin itself is not available, seeds for this fragrant heirloom variety are (see Sources, page 199).

I have been growing this variety at Roughwood off and on since I first bought seeds in the open market at Castelfranco in the early 1970s (and then later introduced the squash to American growers through Seed Savers Exchange). The aroma of sea pumpkins grilled with olive oil and rosemary on barges along the Grand Canal when Venice returns to normal after the tourist season was enchanting. To my mind, *mostarda* made with those big, green, warty pumpkins captures Venice in a jar.

Yield: About 2 quarts (2 liters)

4 pounds (2kg) finely diced pumpkin

¾ cup (4 ounces/125g) Zante currants

1 cup (4 ounces/125g) slivered almonds

¾ cup (4 ounces/125g) candied lemon peel, coarsely chopped

¼ cup (40g) yellow mustard seeds

Grated zest of 1 lemon

1 tablespoon (5g) freshly grated nutmeg, or to taste

2 tablespoons (20g) whole fennel seeds, optional

1½ cups (375g) organic sugar

½ cup (125ml) Dijon mustard (must have creamy texture)

¼ cup (60ml) white wine vinegar

In a steamer basket or colander set over just-boiling water, steam the diced pumpkin until just cooked but still slightly firm, about 15 minutes; do not overcook. Drain any excess liquid and transfer the steamed pumpkin to a large work bowl. Add the currants, almonds, candied lemon peel, mustard seeds, lemon zest, nutmeg, and fennel seeds, if using.

In a small saucepan, combine the sugar with 1 cup (250ml) spring water and set over high heat. Bring to a boil and reduce to a syrup, 5 to 8 minutes. Add the Dijon mustard and vinegar and whisk until smooth. Taste, adjusting the balance of sweet and sour as needed, then pour the hot syrup over the pumpkin mixture and stir.

Without canning, this will keep, covered, in the refrigerator for up to 3 days. To seal, transfer to sterilized jars after adding the syrup and process according to the method on page XX; if you prefer the water bath method, allow 12 minutes. Since the pumpkin is semi-cooked, I don't suggest keeping this longer than 6 months, even stored in a cool, dark place. This pickle is best when freshly made.

Vinaigre Printanier (Spring-Flavored Vinegar)

If it is possible to capture the flavors of spring in a bottle, this charming heirloom recipe from 1809 comes close. The flavor of this vinegar is hard to pin down (just like spring and her moody weather) because much depends on its intensity, meaning the freshness of the several herbs employed. Whatever the mixture, the tarragon and savory should rise above the rest, tempered by the warm complexity of chives, garlic, and shallots.

Every chef has his or her preference for the subtle nuances of one ingredient or the other, and I often add chervil when it is in season. In short, you can fuss over this recipe until the sun freezes, and there will always be room for invention because every spring introduces different challenges. What all classically trained cooks will agree on is that, of all the herb-flavored vinegars now in use (commercially), this is one of the most sophisticated and best made at home. When used sparingly, the vinegar can add subtle character to delicate sauces; when mixed with butter, it imparts ethereal flavors to grilled meat. Once you have it in your pantry, you will guard it like gold and keep the secret that you got it from me. For best results, use oak-aged champagne vinegar; I prefer Napa Valley Naturals because their vinegar is of consistent quality and American made.

Yield: 3½ cups (875ml)

A few sprigs fresh tarragon, to taste

A few sprigs fresh savory, to taste

2 sprigs fresh spearmint

2 sprigs fresh lemon balsam

1 small bunch chives

2 large garlic cloves, cut in half lengthwise

2 large shallots, peeled and cut in half lengthwise

3½ cups (875ml) good-quality champagne vinegar (see headnote)

Sterilize a large bottle in a pot of lightly boiling water and set aside. Pack the herbs, chives, garlic, and shallots into the prepared bottle (use the handle of a wooden spoon to press the ingredients into the bottle). Add the vinegar and close tightly. Let infuse for about 10 days, then strain out the herbs and pour the flavored vinegar into a clean bottle. Seal with a cork or airtight lid and store out of direct sunlight. The vinegar will keep for several years, although I tend to go through it rather quickly, so the best plan is to make it new every spring.

Zucchini Chutney

This recipe is dedicated to those home gardeners who do not know what to do with the bumper crop of baseball bat–size fruit that seems to appear overnight during the height of summer. Drawing inspiration from India, turn overripe squash into spicy chutney that will add zest to your meals throughout the winter. Any firm green squash can be substituted for the zucchini.

Yield: 4 to 5 pints (2 to 2.5 liters)

3½ cups (875g) organic sugar

2½ cups (625ml) red wine vinegar

2 tablespoons (50g) tamarind pulp (picked of seeds or seed fragments)

3½ pounds (1.75kg) mature zucchini, seeded and cut into small dice

2 unripe mangoes (roughly 2 pounds/1kg), peeled and chopped

2 tablespoons (50g) freshly grated ginger

½ cup (90g) minced hot pepper or powdered hot pepper, or to taste

½ cup (175g) toasted unsalted pistachios, coarsely chopped

¼ cup (60g) minced garlic

1 large red onion (8 ounces/500g) cut in half lengthwise, then thinly sliced

½ cup (125ml) virgin (cold-pressed) sesame oil

1½ tablespoons (15g) black mustard seeds

1 tablespoon (10g) whole cumin seeds

In a large saucepan, combine the sugar, vinegar, and tamarind pulp. Set over medium heat and bring to a boil. Cook until reduced to a thin, syrupy consistency, about 20 minutes. While the syrup reduces, combine the zucchini, mangoes, ginger, hot pepper, pistachios, garlic, and onion in a deep work bowl.

Sterilize the jar(s), lid(s), and ring(s) in a saucepan of lightly boiling water and set aside.

In a nonreactive preserving pan large enough to hold all the ingredients, heat the sesame oil over medium heat. Add the mustard seeds and cumin seeds. Once the oil begins to crackle and the seeds start popping, add the zucchini mixture, stirring to coat the ingredients with the hot oil. Add the syrup, then increase the heat to medium-high and cook steadily until thick, about 20 minutes. Transfer to the prepared jars and seal (see page 17).

This will keep for up to 3 years when stored in a cool, dark place; however, it's best consumed within 1 year.

04

Vinegar Infusions

Many years ago, when I was just beginning to explore the world of heritage cookery, I managed to acquire Dr. Thomas Cooper's American edition of *The Domestic Encyclopedia*. The buried treasure in this 1821 magnum opus is Cooper's addendum in volume three devoted to "Domestic Cookery." Dr. Thomas Cooper was indeed a gourmet ahead of his time in many respects, and his advice concerning "vinegars for the storeroom" has always stayed with me. Vinegar infusions are as basic to good cookery as salt, and Dr. Cooper made no secret that tarragon, garlic, shallot, lemon, and pepper vinegar should figure in any well-stocked storeroom inventory. He even sang the virtues of pickled red cabbage (see page 177).

While I soon explored Dr. Cooper's world of cookery and found many of his recipes as trendy as anything served today, it became perfectly clear that his emphasis on the importance of vinegar infusions was a universal truism: Good cookery has always depended on these foundation preparations to carry them forward as matrix flavors on the creative front. On that note, let me be perfectly clear that while my vinegar infusions may echo the classic larders of old-time haute cuisine, good flavor is timeless, and vinegar infusions are like the colors in old master paintings that transcend light: They reflect the taste of their times and mirror the possibilities of the future.

Coriander Vinegar

While seemingly simple, a vinegar flavored with coriander seeds or cilantro leaves, the intense flavor of this preparation should promote it immediately to the ranks of kitchen standbys, especially when cooking with cabbages, or cabbage dishes laced with onions and leeks. Or, taken one step farther, this background flavor is hidden in many Latin and South American recipes, so there is good reason to keep a few bottles at hand to add a hit of bright, herbal freshness.

Yield: About 3 cups (750ml)

Sterilize a 1-quart (1-liter) wide-mouthed jar in boiling water. Add 1 cup (80g) whole coriander seeds or pack the jar half full with cilantro greens. Cover with 3 cups (750ml) white wine vinegar, then close tightly and let stand for 3 weeks in a cool, dark cupboard to infuse. Strain and discard the coriander seeds or greens and rebottle in a clean airtight container. Store with your other household vinegars; for best results, use within 1 year (otherwise the vinegar may oxidize and darken).

Garlic or Shallot Vinegar

If you prefer, omit the bay leaves and increase the amount of garlic to suit your taste—use additional white wine vinegar to adjust the flavor. For Shallot Vinegar, replace the garlic with 6 small shallots, peeled and sliced. Consider this an essential vinegar for your *batterie de cuisine*. Don't cook without it!

Yield: About 3½ cups (875ml)

Sterilize a 1-quart (1-liter) wide-mouthed jar in boiling water. Add 4 large garlic cloves sliced in half lengthwise and 20 fresh bay leaves, lightly bruised (see headnote). Cover with 3½ cups (875ml) white wine vinegar, then close tightly and let stand for 3 weeks in a cool, dark cupboard to infuse. Strain and discard the garlic and bay leaves and rebottle in a clean airtight container. Store with your other household vinegars; for best results, use within 1 year (otherwise the vinegar may oxidize and darken).

Horseradish Vinegar

Horseradish vinegar, with its clean, sharp mustard flavor remains a culinary standby in classic folk cookery. Horseradish or a combination of white pepper and ginger provided medieval spice combinations with heat prior to the introduction of peppers from the New World. Meanwhile, this is one of the oldest and most historically accurate recipes for horseradish vinegar, a condiment in use since the Middle Ages. I make mine with horseradish grown at Roughwood.

Yield: About 3 cups (750ml)

Sterilize a 1-quart (1-liter) wide-mouthed jar in boiling water. Add ¾ cup (100g) peeled and diced horseradish and 3 garlic cloves, sliced in half lengthwise. Cover with 3 cups (750ml) white wine vinegar, then close tightly and let stand for 3 weeks in a cool, dark place. Strain and discard the horseradish and garlic, then rebottle in a clean, airtight container. Store with your other household vinegars; for best results, use within 1 year (otherwise the vinegar may oxidize and darken).

Huacatay Vinegar

There is no comparison when describing the unique flavor of *huacatay*, an herb indigenous to the Andes and an iconic food from the region. Compare its flavor to a combination of tarragon, spearmint, and marigold leaves, plus something extra, making *huacatay* truly something special.

Yield: About 3 cups (750ml)

Sterilize a 1-quart (1-liter) wide-mouthed jar in boiling water. Add 3 cups (225g) *huacatay* leaves, packing them tightly with a wooden potato masher, and 1 thinly sliced onion (about 8 ounces/125g). Cover with 3 cups (750ml) white wine vinegar, then close tightly and let stand for 15 days in a cool, dark place. Strain out the *huacatay* leaves and onion rebottle in a clean, airtight container. Store with your other household vinegars; for best results, use within 1 year (otherwise the vinegar may oxidize and darken).

Green *Shiso* Vinegar

Since this vinegar is used in copious quantities for pickling, it is advisable to make a large batch.

Yield: About 2 quarts (2 liters)

Sterilize a 2-quart (2-liter) wide-mouthed jar in boiling water. Add at least 2 cups (150g) green *shiso* leaves and four or five 2-inch (5-cm) slices fresh ginger. Cover with 1 quart (1 liter) white wine vinegar, then close tightly and let stand for 1 month in a cool, dark place. Strain and discard the *shiso* and ginger, then rebottle in a clean airtight container. Store with your other household vinegars; for best results, use within 1 year (otherwise the vinegar may oxidize and darken).

Red *Shiso* Vinegar

Red *shiso* (sometimes called just *shiso*, and also known colloquially as red perilla or beefsteak plant) was introduced to the Philadelphia region from Japan as a garden ornamental in the 1850s. Since then it has naturalized as a common garden weed whose culinary potential has been appreciated only with the recent wave of interest in Japanese cuisine. From a practical standpoint, red *shiso* vinegar is best made in a large batch of flavored vinegar during the summer, before the *shiso* flowers, this to capture its flavor at its height.

Yield: About 3 cups (750ml)

Sterilize a 1-quart (1-liter) wide-mouthed jar in boiling water. Add 2 cups (150g) red shiso leaves. Cover with 3 cups (750ml) white wine vinegar, then close tightly and let stand for 1 month in a cool, dark cupboard to infuse. Strain and discard the shiso leaves and rebottle in a clean airtight container. Store with your other household vinegars; for best results, use within 1 year (otherwise the vinegar may oxidize and darken).

Raspberry Vinegar

Raspberry vinegar is a key ingredient in the regional cookery of southeastern Pennsylvania, and there are several local companies that make it. Just the same, store-bought is usually expensive, so make your own with ripe berries from a local organic or sustainable farm. I should like to mention that I make raspberry vinegar from yellow (golden), black, and white raspberries. Each has its own special taste and can produce delicious results when used in pickles; for example, use fruity black raspberry vinegar to add an interesting new dimension to Sweet and Sour Plums (page 136), and delicate, floral white raspberry vinegar is truly ethereal when introduced to Apple Chutney (page 122).

Yield: About 1 quart (1 liter)

Sterilize a 2-quart (2-liter) wide-mouthed jar in boiling water. Add 8 ounces (250g) freshly picked raspberries, caps removed. Cover with 1 quart (1 liter) red wine vinegar (6 percent acidity), then close tightly and let stand for 1 month in a cool, dark place. Strain through a jelly bag and discard the solids, then rebottle the strained vinegar in a clean airtight container. Store with your other household vinegars. It should keep indefinitely but may begin to oxidize after 2 years; for best results, make each year as raspberries come into season.

Sources

This list aims to provide the home gardener–home pickler with trustworthy sources for growing varieties of heirloom produce named in this book. Some may be available in local farmers' markets, depending on where you live, while others are actually quite rare. Where mature trees are required for fruit, such as for blood peaches or Cornelian cherries, your best source is One Green World (**onegreenworld.com**).

Bamboo

As an ingredient, bamboo can prove frustrating unless you're familiar with it, because information on cooking with freshly harvested shoots is hard to find. Complicating matters, there are more than one thousand species of bamboo found in Asia, Africa, and Central and South America. Theoretically, while all bamboo shoots are edible when properly prepared, the growth and shape of bamboo is heavily influenced by environment and sensitivity to frost. For this reason, shoots can vary in size from something resembling baby asparagus to monsters as large around as a basketball. Furthermore, the number of shoots suitable for pickling will depend on the type of bamboo you are using, the age of the grove, and the soil—because the fatter the young shoots, the better. Many ornamental varieties produce long, stringy shoots not suitable for pickling.

Regardless of size, from a nutritional standpoint, bamboo shoots are roughly equivalent to onions, while their flavor is akin to artichokes. The shoots, or culms, are covered with a sheath resembling cornhusks that must be peeled away (this will reduce the weight of each shoot by at least half). This amount of waste is why the moso or timber bamboo (*Phyllostachys edulis*) is favored as a source for commercial bamboo shoots. Moso shoots are large and provide cooks with good yields of tender inner shoots *after* peeling. Unfortunately, moso varieties are climate-sensitive and will only grow in the southeastern United States. Fishing Pole bamboo (*Phyllostachys aurea*) is the best alternative for American gardeners—and the variety used in these recipes—because it also produces large shoots but will grow in most parts of the United States warmer than zone 5. Given the amount of waste when processing bamboo shoots, the best course of action usually is to harvest (or purchase) more than you think you will need, whichever variety you choose.

Fishing Pole bamboo
Ty Ty Plant Nursery
tytyga.com

Beans

Beurre de Rocquencourt bush, Jackson Wonder bush lima
Baker Creek Heirloom Seeds
rareseeds.com

Hebron's Tenderette bush, Landreth Stringless bush, Sadie's baby lima
Roughwood Seed Collection
roughwoodtable.org

Marrowfat bush or white marrowfat bush, Pencil Pod black wax bush
Victory Seed Company
victoryseeds.com

Beets

Bull's Blood
Baker Creek Heirloom Seeds
rareseeds.com

Early Blood Turnip
Monticello
monticelloshop.org

Cabbage

Early Etampes cabbage
(also called Cuore di Bue)
Baker Creek Heirloom Seeds
rareseeds.com

Cannonball cabbage, *karam saag*
(Kashmiri collards)
Roughwood Seed Collection
roughwoodtable.org

Crab Apples

Callaway crab apple
One Green World
onegreenworld.com

Index

(Page references in *italics* refer to illustrations.)

Acknowledgments

This book has been a work in progress for so many years that frankly I cannot remember when I first thought to write it. Each summer and fall were crowded with pickling experiments; the recipes simply accumulated and many of the best are now preserved between the covers of this book. My literary agent Lisa Ekus believed in this project as soon as I mentioned it to her, and I give her top credit for taking it to Rizzoli because it is a perfect match.

 My Rizzoli editor, Jono Jarrett, is not only fun to work with, he is gifted with a special vision which he brought to the book, and once here at Roughwood, he understood why that name should be in the title. My food reflects the spirit of the house, and Noah Fecks captured that ephemeral magic in his photographs. I owe them both—Jono and Noah—thanks for two memorable weeks of hard work behind the camera, yes, even down on the floor of the old tavern room where Roughwood's ethereal light seems to capture the imagination of every photographer who sees it.

I should also like to mention Alain Passard who has always been an inspiration to me. His way with heirloom vegetables at Arpège cannot be imitated. Perhaps it is the wavy Lalique windows throwing their Zen-like light into the restaurant, the simple fragrance of a rare beet well cooked; whatever, Chef Passard has a way of bringing his farms into his kitchen and turning that fusion of rustic truth into a Parisian reality.

Lastly, I want to acknowledge my late grandmother, Grace Hickman Weaver (1900–1997), who was my culinary mentor and best friend. I still miss her because she could hold forth for hours over the qualities of freshly harvested cucumbers, which variety of green tomato was "just so" for a good pickle, or the correct hand motions for squeezing cabbage for pepper hash. She was a living encyclopedia of culinary experience, but it was her golden hands that taught me how to transform vegetables into art.